Restitution

Sheila Smith

Sheila Smith.

Sequel to

Valley of Stone

Rural Haven

R E S T I T U T I O N

Copyright © Sheila Smith 2010

All rights reserved

ISBN : 978-184426-903-7

First published 2010 by Fastprint of Peterborough

Printed by
www.printondemand-worldwide.com

Characters from Rural Haven

John Birkett Senior
John Birkett Jnr m Marjorie Jones
Children Mary, Harold Benjamin, Jane, Johnny

Mary is married to DI David Waring, they have a son Mark
Jane Birkett is married to Mark Richards-Fleming, have
daughter Janice Joan

Harold Jones Senior, wife Janie

Evan Evans married Sarah Birkett
Children Evan John, Sarah Kate (twins), Megan (Megs)
Sarah Kate m Jerome Graham

Robbie Birkett m Jessie Williams
Daughter Jessica Hope

Megan Birkett (sister of Evan, widow of Matthew)
Daughters Charlotte and Shirley
Megan Birkett married Joe Fleming, adopted boys Mark,
Andrew & Tony Richards, after the death of their mother.

Williams Families.
Daniel Williams Senr – wife Jessie
Son Daniel m Rachel Scott (evacuee) she had daughter
Samantha & son James, and their son Daniel
Daughter Jess m Robbie Birkett, daughter Hope
Ezekiel Williams brother to Dan Senr, wife Emily
Son Ezekiel, daughter Ruth, (son Luke deceased)
Ruth in partnership with Paolo Romano, they have son
Giovanni and daughter Emily Maria.

Ezekiel m Charity (now deceased)
Children Micheal and Elizabeth.
Zeke is engaged to Megs Birkett

Reg Ridgely has come to the valley with Johnny Birkett.
Reg is engaged to Hope Birkett

Ben Field and his wife Jenny nee Birkett
Children Katy and adopted son Benjamin

Remaining evacuee.
Sandra Harvey who has returned to the valley.

RESTITUTION by Sheila Smith

This novel tells the story of Sarah Kate Evans, who together with her twin brother Evan John Evans, join the Women's Auxiliary Air Force and Royal Air Force, in late 1939. They serve during World War Two, he as a pilot in the RAF, and she becomes a Special Operations Executive (S.O.E.).

This is a novel mainly about Sarah Kate Evans and her twin Evan John, but brought into the story are some family characters from the two previous books, set in Langdale, in the English Lake District.

I dedicate Restitution to my late parents John Brynmore Jones born in the Langdale Valley, and my mother Elsie Jones (nee Kitchin). Also my brother Roy, who went to Australia and worked all over the Far East, my brother David who joined the RAF and saw the world with his wife Jean, and their children Roy and Michelle, all of whom keep returning to the valley. Also our stepmother Muriel Jones who lived in the valley for many years, and half-sister Jennifer Grummert, who together with her husband Kerry and their daughter Morgane live in Switzerland.

RESTITUTION

CHAPTER ONE

Twins, Evan John and Sarah Kate Evans were both deep in thought as they sat with their backs to the engine, whilst listening to the clickity-clack of the train wheels on the rails. There was an elderly couple on the seats opposite to them, and a woman with two unruly children, who kept moving about in the other four seats. Sarah wondered why the children had not been evacuated like the ones taken from the North East, to her parent's home in the Lake District. Sarah also wondered where these people could possibly be travelling, as there were no signs on the station platforms, and it was late nineteen thirty nine, and there was a War on! Her own thoughts were a bit chaotic and she believed those of Evan John too, as he kept crossing and re-crossing his legs and tapping his forefinger on his raised knee.

She sighed, and patted Evan John's arm, she knew she was biased being his twin, but he was rather a nice person, and handsome with it. "You needn't worry Evan. I may be only a *girl* but I am allowed to live my own life as I please.

1

Dad and mam will accept my decision and I would not have made a very good land-girl anyway. I *would* have to do something different like you as we have lived in the country all our lives, until the last two years. Also our Megs will be fit to burst. It was really strange how we decided to volunteer, and then you got your call-up papers two days later." She smiled thinking about their younger sister Megan, who was always writing, painting, or rushing around the valley.

"Mam and dad might agree with our decision, but I bet you Great Grandma Kate will be spitting feathers when she hears that you have joined up, you could be a land-girl or get some sort of war work." His sister looked really well, and was being eyed up by the elderly man opposite, who was looking at her, not directly, but was watching her reflection in the train window, and as usual Sarah Kate didn't notice this!

"Great Grandma Kate will be expecting it to be as bad as World War One, but it can't possibly be like that. She didn't think I should go to university, but she came around to it in the end, now she is quite proud of us both."

"I guess we will get separated, but I hope it won't be too soon," Evan said worriedly.

"You want to fly and so do I, so maybe we will be together for quite a while," Sarah replied hopefully. She had never been separated from her twin, and knew that it would seem like part of her was missing, they were used to seeing each other at least every few days. This they had managed at university, although Sarah Kate was taking languages, and Evan John, after a long debate was studying physics and maths.

Evan was not sure what he thought about his twin's ambitions, he doubted very much that she would get into flying so easily. Although they had heard that women pilots were sometimes used to ferry planes to where they were needed. He believed they had already had some luck, as the Women's Auxiliary Air Force where Sarah was going was on the same RAF Station that he would be joining. They might be together for at least basic training.

"Have you been counting the station stops Evan, I think we should get out at the next?" Sarah asked, starting to collect her belongings. It was so cold that they were wearing as much as possible, and that left them with only one bag each. Evan nodded, stood up and fastened his overcoat. Soon they would be dressed in the RAF blue, and *he* couldn't wait, but in a way he wished that Sarah Kate was not such an intrepid young woman, he would have preferred to think of her somewhere safe.

As the train slowed down, he dropped down the door window and peered out. "This could be it," he said briskly, and just before he stepped onto the platform when the train had stopped, the elderly gentleman who had been sitting opposite to them looked up.

"Good luck to you young people," he said wearily. Sarah looked at him with a brief smile, and noticed tears in his eyes. Like their dad, he had probably been in the last war, but he was much older than her dad. She was relieved that their dad was *just* too old to be called up for this war, which would have been unlikely anyway, as he still had a piece of shrapnel lodged near to his heart, from the last war.

They managed to get a lift with a local coal merchant with two young men, who had joined them on the platform, full of excitement and eagerness. They all arrived at the RAF base quivering with excitement - which would hopefully dislodge some of the coal dust now attached to their clothes!

Within ten minutes of arriving at the base, Sarah Kate was directed to a large room, where a number of young women were queuing for a medical, this was followed by a trip to the wash rooms, and then they were provided with W.A.A.F. Regulation uniforms and bedding. They were directed to their wooden built hut, and they were told to store away their bounty, consisting of a knife, fork, spoon and enamel mug, and then to clean their space, and those spaces used for communal use. Her spirits had dropped when she watched Evan John move off in the opposite direction with his two new acquaintances, and they were still low. She pulled herself together as she noticed two young girls with tears in their eyes, it seemed to her that already their high expectations had not been fulfilled, or they were already homesick. Sarah was determined to learn to fly – she would remain focused on that dream, and as yet this had not been denied her!

Later, she sat on the iron framed bed with metal springs, and thin mattress, that she had just made up herself, and she was now dressed in regulation pyjamas which were at least in comfortable cotton, shivering after a cool shower. There were six beds in the room, three empty with the thin mattresses rolled up, and her own and those of Mary (that was all they had managed to find out from her as she was missing her family) and that of Tina Trevor who was bemoaning the fact that she didn't have any curling tongs, and most of her make-up had been taken away from her. Tina glanced across at Sarah with a disgruntled look. "It's alright for you Sarah Kate, you look quite pale and interesting without any make-up, but I need it, it's not easy looking this good all the time." She shrugged when Sarah gave her a brief smile and raised her eyebrows in disbelief. Tina continued as she brushed her hair, which fell in a bob just below her ears. "I joined up to get a young pilot to marry me. When this war is over they will still need pilots, and we'll be set up for life."

"I do hope you are right Tina, and that the war finishes before we *lose* most of them, good luck to you and to them," Sarah Kate finished with a sigh, her heart dropped as she thought of the danger her twin might be in shortly. "Don't forget to remove your nail polish, or you could possibly be up on a charge in the morning. Six thirty I think they said we'd be wakened up."

Tina pulled a face in disgust and started on her bright red nails. "Why do you have a double barrelled name Sarah Kate? A bit posh for a lass from the countryside isn't it?"

"Just call me Sarah if you want. My mother is Sarah, and my great grandma is Kate, as is my cousin, so I'm stuck with both names at home, it's less confusing."

"What sort of work did you do Sarah, before coming here?"

"I was at university taking languages. What did you do Tina?"

"Well, so you are posh Sarah *Kate*, and you wouldn't want to *know* what I did." She finished with her nails, and relaxed in her bed and pulled the bedcover over her head, leaving Sarah wondering if they were friends or not!

Sarah looked at the light switch at the end of the room, and then glanced at Mary, who had also covered her head, but her shoulders were shaking and Sarah was certain she was crying. She patted Mary's shoulder, she hoped comfortingly, and when Mary whispered 'Goodnight Sarah' Sarah went to switch off the light.

Over the next three weeks filled with basic training, the other beds in the room were filled with young hopefuls. Everyone seemed to get on very well, but Sarah still gave a helping hand to Mary, and enjoyed her confrontations, now quite friendly, with Tina.

One day Sarah was hurrying to get back to the barracks to help Mary get herself ready as she was to go for a second medical examination, when she was stopped on her way by a distinguished looking RAF Officer with grey at his temples, and he *spoke* to her much to her surprise. "What is your ambition young woman with regard to the W.A.A.F?" He asked with speculation narrowing his eyes. She noticed his insignia showed that he was a Wing Commander.

"To fly Sir as soon as possible, like my brother," she answered promptly, after saluting. She raised her eyes in surprise, as his question had been asked in French, and she had automatically answered likewise.

"Private Sarah Kate Evans?"

"Yes Sir."

"It is unlikely that you will be taught to fly private." He said in English, and walked along with his hands clasped behind his back, his head bowed in deep thought.

Damn Sarah thought - had she been too pushy? It seemed that he knew of Evan John, and she truly hoped that Evan would be given the chance to fly – women still seemed to be second class citizens although they now had the vote! She hoped that she would get a chance to find Evan John and find out what was happening in his life, also she just needed to make sure that he was safe and well, although something inside her believed that he was, but this opportunity did not arise. Both Sarah and Tina had been informed that they would probably be trained as Code and Cipher Officers, and although Sarah was intrigued by this idea, she was not overjoyed, as she still hoped for an opportunity to learn to fly, although she now had learned that the W.A.A.F did not actually teach women to fly! She later learned that the British Air Transport Auxiliary were women flyers who had volunteered to ferry aircraft for the Royal Air Force and Royal Navy in wartime Britain, and they must have come into the service able to fly, or were classed as a separate entity.

Two weeks later Sarah was on a train travelling north. They were not sure of their destination, but accompanying her were three RAF men, one of whom was a sergeant. The sergeant seemed to be very strict, with very little to say, except to keep them in line. He appeared to be dozing in the corner of the compartment.

"Hey, Miss, do you know where we are going, and why?" the younger of the two men asked under his breath. "We seem to be going the wrong way for the war."

Sarah shook her head, and returned his enquiring glance. "Do you speak French, German or Italian?" she asked, her mind going into overdrive, as she hadn't been able to get the officer out of her mind who had spoken to her in French two weeks ago. She wondered if it had been some sort of test. Her languages at university were French and German, and she had also studied Latin at grammar school.

"Only a bit of French, I was learning to be a gym instructor." He tightened the muscles in his square shoulders and strong arms to prove his point, but looked confused, and glanced towards the sergeant who moved and stretched his arms above his head as though he had just awakened, but Sarah thought he had not been asleep at all.

"Quiet in the ranks, get some sleep, you'll get little in the next couple of weeks," the Sergeant said grumpily. This silenced them, and gave them plenty to think about for the rest of the journey.

Sarah had recognised Gretna Green when they had passed near the small town. Her interest in that part of the country was because her parents married there, before her dad had gone to fight in the 1914-1918 War. They passed Gretna nearly two hours ago, and she reckoned that they must be almost at the top of the Great Glen, near Inverness, when the train eventually came to a stop, and they were told to leave the carriage. They were put into a military armoured car, and driven on to a large country house. It was dark now, and Sarah was really tired, and hoped they would be allowed to eat and sleep very soon.

She wondered how Mary and Tina were doing, and regretted the fact that she had not been given an opportunity to say goodbye to them. She hoped that Tina would take Mary under her wing for a while, as she was slowly coming out of her shell and didn't cry nearly so much as previously, and would benefit a lot from her time in the W.A.A.F. Just as she hoped to do herself, now that she had realised that she was being groomed for something, and only time would tell what that was!

The two RAF men were given a room, and Sarah was pleased to find that she had a small room to herself under the eves of the house with a tiny window. When they went to the dining room to eat they were surprised to find ninety to a hundred people in there. However, there was very little banter or talking of any description. After eating and trudging upstairs, Sarah had a nice warm bath and an early night, wondering what would be happening tomorrow, all she knew was that they would be awakened before seven for an early breakfast.

She was already awake when someone hammered on her door, and she was quickly dressed warmly in woollen trousers and shirt and sweater, these had already been in her room. Last evening they had been told not to wear their uniforms.

She had almost finished her porridge oats, served without sugar or milk, only a dash of salt, when the two RAF men joined her.

"I can't stand this, not being able to call anyone by name," the younger one complained, "and I can't eat this porridge stuff." He glanced up to find the Sergeant standing behind him.

"Eat it lad, and some bacon, or you'll not get through the day. In a couple of days you'll be looking forward to it! When you've finished, go into that room over there and take a backpack and anything else you think you will need for the day. We are going on a long hike. Be outside in fifteen minutes."

Sarah had glanced out of the bedroom window earlier, although it was still quite dark, and realised the terrain was very like that of the Lake District, but much bigger, but imagined that the weather would be just as changeable.

The day started frosty and bright, and Sarah found it a joy to be walking in the hills once more. It was not long before the young RAF man was suffering from blisters on his feet, he blamed his walking books, but the Sergeant swore that they had been fitted properly, and he was just not used to walking so far. Sarah was allowed to provide him with some plasters from her first aid kit, but when it was found that one of the men had a compass and no map, and the other a map and no compass they were left to find their own way back to Base. Only one of them had thought to bring weatherproof over-trousers and, of course, it did rain very heavily. The only thing that Sarah lacked was a bar of chocolate to keep her going, but she had not liked to take some from the small pile in the room where they had been instructed to help themselves, as she didn't have any ration coupons!

About mid afternoon the Sergeant was following his group of three at a distance, observing their decisions and attitudes, and he was not surprised that the two men had decided to follow Sarah and had caught up with her. She looked warm and dry and they looked wet and uncomfortable. Suddenly he saw Sarah stop, she stared up into the sky for at least a minute, and then she held her hand to her chest and bent her knees. The Sergeant thought she

9

must be ill, and hurried forward, he had heard of even the young and fit having heart attacks or blood vessels bursting. He reached her side and put his hand on her elbow.

"Are you alright Evans," he asked his voice anxious. "Sorry I forgot no names."

She stared at him for a moment realising that someone did know her name, and the group was, in fact, being monitored.

"I'm fine thank you Sergeant. It's my twin, he is learning to be a fighter pilot at least I think he is." She straightened up slowly. "Now I know he is. He just had a near miss, but it's alright now, he's fine," Sarah replied, taking a deep thankful breath. The Sergeant looked back at the young woman, and hoped that nothing happened to *her* whilst her twin was *flying*, or anything could happen!

The two young RAF men did not have a very good day and Sarah did. However, the next day they were to do an obstacle course through the forest. The men did best at this, but Sarah did quite well, but was not so quick on the things that needed a short burst of energy and physical strength. When they started going out for a five mile run, she surprised herself, and was soon looking forward to this pleasant form of exercise, on a regular basis. She was surprised at herself, it felt wonderful to be fit, energetic and well.

Strangely, at the beginning of June everything seemed to be suspended. Sarah was advised that she could either stay where she was, or go back to base for a few days. She decided to go back to her base, in the hope that she would be able to see Evan John. The strange feelings she had experienced on the hills still haunted her, and she needed to know that he was alright. The two RAF men decided to do the same, but they were all advised that they should keep their mouths shut, and explanations would be forthcoming if they completed their course. With the Sergeant's agreement she was able to send a message to Evan advising him of her time of arrival at the train station. She had been advised that she could not tell her brother what she was doing, but she was longing to see him, and was bitterly disappointed after a long train journey when he met her off the train, to find that he had two friends with him. She had selfishly wanted to have her brother to herself, after being parted for so long, and was slightly put out that he seemed to be enjoying the company of his friends.

CHAPTER TWO

Sarah and her companions were once again wearing their uniforms, and within seconds of stepping onto the station platform, Sarah was swung into her brother's arms and twirled around. Her cap was dislodged and her dark blond hair was unpinned and swung around her shoulders in disarray, catching the sunlight.

"Evan John put me down," she demanded with a laugh, and was placed on her feet carefully, and she stood back and looked at the two young men with him, trying not to show too plainly her disappointment!

"This is my sister Sarah Kate. Sarah I'd like you to meet Brian and Jerome. Brian and I have just learned to fly Spitfires, and soon we'll be as good as Jerome."

Brian shook her hand lightly, looking embarrassed but unable to take his eyes of her lovely face, and shining eyes when they looked at her brother.

She turned to Jerome who put her cap and two hairpins into her left hand, and then took her right hand in both of his. She looked a long way up into dark eyes which held her gaze and made her feel decidedly odd. He slowly let go of her hand and turned to Evan.

"Hey Evan, I kinda like you, but I think the female side of the Evans clan is even more eye-catching." His strange American accent seemed to grate against her nerves, but she could still feel where his confident hands had held hers.

She looked at the two men with whom she had travelled down from Scotland, and acknowledged them as they were walking passed. "See you in three days here." She pointed down to the platform, and they smiled.

"Yes Miss. See you in three days, two-thirty p.m."

"Have you already got a date Sarah Kate," Jerome asked annoyingly. "Where are you going in three days at 14.30 hours?"

"No - and it's my business. Jerome was that your name?"

"You know it is," Evan said. "We planned to take you for some lunch, and then I thought we would ring home together. We'll leave it until later when Megs will be home from grammar school."

"That's a lovely idea Evan John." Sarah said, and they turned and walked out of the station and towards The Royal Oak, a public house which advertised lunches. They found a table and all sat down, and Sarah wondered if it would have been better if Jerome had sat down beside her, as she continually felt his eyes on her from across the table. She thought she had discouraged him from using his flirtatious banter on her by being abrupt a few minutes ago but that was not the case. He seemed unfazed, and even more intrigued. She decided to ignore Jerome, and glanced at her brother who was looking particularly happy at the moment.

"I knew you were flying Evan, but will you please be more careful in future, you spoiled my afternoon a few days ago, the Sergeant thought I was ill."

Evan looked regretful, Brian looked confused, and Jerome stared at her in amazement, his gaze keen and interested. Sarah Kate wished she hadn't said anything!

"Jerome put me right, and everything was alright Sarah," Evan said apologetically.

"What gives," Jerome said staring across at Sarah, and then to Evan.

"Sarah is my twin, as well as my sister." Evan said.

"Well, I guess that *sort* of explains it," Jerome said shaking his head.

"Why did *you* have to *put Evan right*?" Sarah asked, slightly irritated by Evan's confident friend.

"Jerome has been flying for years. He *volunteered* to fly with the RAF, he came over especially to do that, he is from Canada," Evan John quickly interrupted.

"That explains his strange accent," Sarah said without thinking.

"Is that so," Jerome said, and she could see that she had annoyed him. He looked angry, and Evan looked anything but pleased, and Brian slightly embarrassed.

"What I meant was, I was wondering why there was a nuance of a *French* accent here and there," Sarah said. She decided not to apologise to him, he was too full of himself anyway! "I wonder why we've been given a few days off, from the course we were on." She mused, trying to change the subject.

"Probably because of what is going on over in Dunkirk, there is a big evacuation of the expeditionary force troops taking place from the shores of Dunkirk, together with French and Belgian troops. A huge fleet of destroyers, ferries, fishing boats and even river cruisers are taking part. There could be a big loss of life," Jerome said regretfully. Suddenly he stood up from the table. "Sorry Evan, it doesn't seem right us sitting here drinking tea, I'm going back to base."

"Jerome, you know we can't fly *all* the time, we need rest." Evan replied.

Jerome moved off from the table and then turned back. "Do you speak French too Sarah Kate, seeing as *you know* all about my *strange* accent?" She nodded and felt really upset, why couldn't she keep her big mouth shut? He then continued, "probably German too?"

"Yes, I'm sorry I didn't mean to be rude about your accent." She felt quite small and a bit stupid.

"There's a War on Sarah, I'm not at all bothered about you thinking you have said the wrong thing. Be careful Sarah, take care, or *you* will be upsetting Evan, whilst he is *flying*!" He walked away towards the door, with Brian following making apologetic signs to Evan and Sarah.

Sarah felt the teapot, and then poured some lukewarm tea into her cup, just for something to do. The silence at the table was becoming too long.

"Don't you like Jerome? I think it's a wonderful thing he has done, volunteering to fly with the RAF, he is a brilliant pilot. He doesn't *have* to put his life in danger, and he could now be nice and safe in Canada with his family."

"I'm not sure what I feel about Jerome, except that I certainly can't ignore him. Talking of family, I think we should get back to base and try to contact them by telephone, as I've only written about once a week, it will be nice to speak to them. You haven't told them at home that we have joined up have you Evan? When we go home again will be soon enough. We don't want them to worry."

"No of course not, they will know soon enough, and when that time arrives hopefully I will be a fully fledged pilot, and they need not worry quite so much. What are you going to tell them about what your doing Sarah?"

"Nothing just yet, I started as a Code and Cipher Officer, as I still am some of the time, so that will do. I don't know for certain what I'll be doing, and like you, they needn't worry about that yet. They must wonder why we haven't written home as often as usual." Sarah said, knowing that they both had their own ideas about what she would be doing, but neither wanted to mention it!

Later they both spoke with their parents and sister Megs, and were made aware of what was happening in their home valley. Sarah was interested in hearing everything from Megs, who made it all seem quite exciting. She was shocked to learn that her cousin Mary's boyfriend, Luke Williams had joined the Border Regiment, as he was a farm worker and could have stayed at home. After basic training he had returned home for a few days leave, and he and Mary had married. Sarah was looking forward to meeting the Maitland twins who had been evacuated to the valley, and were keeping Megs occupied and giving their mother plenty to do. She felt quite tearful when they had to say goodbye, and vowed to write home more often.

That evening Brian escorted her to The Royal Oak, where he informed her, the local RAF lads usually came for a drink. It would be quite entertaining. Unfortunately both Evan and Jerome were having an early night, as they were flying early in the morning. She liked Brian very much, and she tried to make the evening enjoyable, and thought she succeeded fairly well. There was a lot of singing, and drinking, and everyone was strenuously ignoring the fact that there was a war on!

The next day when Evan contacted her, he was tired and uncommunicative for quite a while, and she told him she needed some exercise, and they took a long walk, around five miles, and she could see that he was feeling much better on their return. She was aware that she would not see him again before she had to leave for Scotland, but she knew that they had both enjoyed this time together, but would have to get used to not seeing each other for weeks or months at a time.

The next day she enjoyed a long walk, and did a little shopping, which was a waste of time as she didn't know what she would be doing in the weeks ahead. She was early at the railway station and settled down to read a newspaper, waiting for the two RAF men to join her for their journey north.

She glanced at the station clock, it was two o'clock, or was it fourteen hundred hours? Why had she had to think about that handsome but arrogant Canadian with the irritating – everything! He had entered her mind yesterday too.

"Hi Sarah Kate." She put the paper down on her knee, and stared at Jerome in surprise, he was folding his long frame to sit on the bench next to her.

"Is Evan coming?" she asked in surprise. Her heart was beating fast, and she took a deep breath, feeling rather confused.

"No, he won't make it in time, as he was just landing as I left the base."

Sarah was disappointed, but couldn't take her eyes off Jerome, he looked sure of himself and determined. She raised her eyebrows as he looked into her wide enquiring eyes. Why was he here, because Evan John wasn't?

"Damn it. Your colleagues have just arrived on the platform. They are nice enough guys, but they should know that you are off limits. I may not see you again Sarah Kate, and I have been wondering what it would be like to kiss you, so I think to stop those guys from bothering you and to keep me from eternally wondering, I think I should......." Jerome put his hands on her shoulders and turned her towards him and put his lips to hers in a brief kiss, and then he took a breath and kissed her more thoroughly. The train came into the station, and they both stood – he took two steps away, then two steps back, put his arms around her and hugged her, whispering in her ear, his breath warm "better than I could ever have imagined" before walking briskly away and through the gates of the station.

Her mind seemed to have gone blank, and she put her fingers to her sensitive lips in surprise, and then with a bemused smile joined her colleagues on the train. This particular journey north did not seem nearly as long as the previous one. As soon as she had first met Jerome she had taken a dislike to him considering him to be too sure of himself and rather arrogant. Was that true or was it just to cover up the strange attraction she had felt towards him, and was it possible that he felt the same? Upon arrival in the north of Scotland she was anxious to get her meal over, and get to bed in order to let her over active mind assimilate her chaotic feelings, which was probably pointless as when she next saw Evan John, Jerome could be with another squadron trying to instil confidence in other new flyers!

Sarah and her colleagues were kept very busy, as the next three weeks were taken up with more outdoor exercise, but there were also unarmed combat sessions, map reading, field craft and basic signalling (the use of wireless communications). When elementary demolition and explosives handling started, Sarah had a good idea what all this training was about? She was amazed at the tools and gadgets that could be provided for their use – strange things like a special gun that could be hidden up a sleeve, and an exploding suitcase, or even an exploding rat, which looked amazingly like the real thing! She began to wonder why they were not advised what they were training for, something obviously undercover, perhaps in an occupied country she was beginning to believe. Did they have an option, or would they be forced to use the knowledge and training they had acquired?

One afternoon she spent four hours speaking French with four of her colleagues, and found this very easy as her grasp of the language had come easily to her. The afternoon speaking only German was much harder, and by the end of it she felt exhausted, and convinced that she had a lot to learn. It would have been much easier to become a land girl!

She learned to shoot a Colt .45 and .38, tucking her firing arm into her hip, and firing off two shots to make sure of hitting the target. However, it was the small lethal fighting knife that she thought she would never be able to use on another living being. That week she asked to see the chaplain, as she had seen one about wearing a dog-collar. She was worried about the ethical ramifications of this type of warfare, it was rather different from looking your enemy in the eye and going on from there, on an equal footing, and may the best man or woman win! However, before this could be arranged she and five of her colleagues were told to pack up their things, as they would be moving to a place near Manchester in the morning.

When they arrived they realised that they were on an aerodrome, and all at once realised that they would be learning to parachute from an aeroplane. Sarah was determined not to fail at this juncture of her training, and in the end found it very exciting although terrifying. However, they did not progress to an actual parachute jump from a plane, but were advised that when and if this did take place, they would be doing it from a height of only three hundred to four hundred feet. A truly terrifying thought!

Their last port of call was to a house in the country, where they were herded into a large room, where a panel of

RAF, WAAF, and two civilians were seated, who were introduced as experts in all forms of covert and irregular warfare. Sarah looked around her, and realised that not everyone she had come across on the various courses were there, some must have fallen at the wayside during the months of training. The ones who were there she did not know by name, and was glad, she did not want to put any of her colleagues at risk should she meet them again in different, and more dangerous circumstances.

The remaining group were told in great detail about the brief history of the Special Operations Executive (S.O.E.). They were advised of the covert and clandestine warfare in which they would be expected to participate and of the benefits of 'resistance movements' in occupied countries, and how these could often enable the smooth advance movements by invading forces.

Sarah was then moved South near to the WAAF Base she had left. She was given a room in a large country house, and was advised that this was a centre for housing Special Operations Executives, and they would be allowed to visit their families, but their location would be, of necessity, secret. Sarah went back to her Code and Cipher work in this same location and waited. She no longer insisted on speaking with a chaplain, as she now wanted to prove to herself that she could do what she had been trained for! Her motivation and determination was reinforced after a telephone conversation with her mother Sarah and sister Megs. The young Luke Williams had been killed at Dunkirk, and her cousin Mary was devastated, as they had just married and she was pregnant with his child. Sarah vaguely remembered him at school, he was a few years younger, and she felt for his parents, his sister Ruth, and brother Zeke, who must be devastated. Sarah felt sick as she remembered that she had been visiting Evan John, and had met Jerome at that time, little knowing that one of the young men from home had been killed during those few days. Every life lost was a tragedy, but knowing and remembering one, and his older siblings very well as a small child, brought it home to her with a definite sting in the tail. Something had to be done to put a stop to this barbaric warfare, how many countries and ethnic originals were going to be drawn in to this bizarre situation? According to the newspapers and news bulletins the beaches of Dunkirk were littered with decaying bodies and the twisted shapes of hundreds of battered vehicles. Also weapons littered the lanes along which the retreating army marched, including British, French and Belgian troops.

CHAPTER THREE

Sarah had four days leave, and set off for the railway station as soon as she heard. She needed to spend some time with her parents and family, in the valley which had been her home for most of her life. After about half an hour spent on the train she picked up her small suitcase, and waited until the train slowed down at the next station. She stood on the platform for a few seconds, and then she felt a tap on her shoulder.

"Sarah Kate, we'd better get back on the train," Evan said with a broad smile, as he opened a carriage door, and waited for her to precede him into the carriage. "I've got a three day pass, and decided to go home, and I guess you have done the same? I had a feeling you were on the train a few minutes ago."

They settled down in the carriage which only had two other occupants, who eyed their uniforms, and looked at them with respectful glances.

"I have four days Evan, but don't say anything to the family - we will both travel back together. We might never get time off together for a long time, and we should make the most of it." Sarah said with a smile. She had a strange feeling, and realised that she would have been pleased if Evan had brought Jerome along with him. Very strange, as she was still of the opinion that he was arrogant and too sure of himself! "Are your immediate colleagues Brian and Jerome safe and well," she heard herself asking, and wondered where the question had come from, but was relieved when Evan replied that they were!

After an uneventful journey north to Windermere station, after changing trains twice, they moved on to a bus to Ambleside, and from there the last part of their journey, another bus to the valley. They knew most of the people on the Langdale valley bus, and were excitedly accompanied to Rowan Trees, and they both knew that it would not be long before the rest of the family found out that they had arrived and would be hell-bent on joining them.

Evan Evans welcomed his son home, and proudly surveyed him in his RAF uniform. He had not mentioned to his wife Sarah that he believed, although he and his twin were at university, that Evan John would still be called up. Sarah looked shocked, but pulled Evan John around towards her and with a sinking feeling, full of love, and she hugged her only son to her with a silent prayer for his safe return.

Both Evan and Sarah were astounded as Sarah Kate came into the living room followed by her excited sister Megs.

"Look mam, look dad, Evan John and Sarah Kate volunteered, and then Evan got his papers calling him up. Isn't it fantastic, I hope I can join-up eventually, maybe I'll be a war correspondent like Winston Churchill used to be," Megs looked at her parents and saw a myriad of expressions crossing their faces – horror, shock, pride and love. Megs sighed deeply, and continued "but I guess by the time I'm old enough the war will be over."

Evan pulled his eldest daughter towards him for a long hug, and Sarah saw her husband's eyes over Sarah Kate's shoulder. He was devastated as she was herself, but by the time he looked at his daughter there was no sign of it. They were twins and had done most things together, but this was hard to take, why hadn't Sarah Kate decided to do war work, or to be a land girl? Sarah glanced at her excited youngest daughter, who had already realised that this excitement would not last for long!

"Megs, go and fetch Bernard and Brenda to meet your brother and sister." She glanced at Evan John and Sarah Kate. "They too are twins, thirteen now, and we are certain they will also be going to university eventually. You should meet them before the rest of the family arrive."

Bernard shook hands gravely with Evan John and, thereafter, followed him around asking searching questions at every opportunity. Brenda smiled and allowed her brother to take the lead, following at a respectful pace but taking everything in that was being said.

Five minutes later the rest of the family did arrive, Great Grandma Kate, Granddad John, Uncle John and his wife Marjorie, Uncle Matthew and his wife Megan, and cousins (who were not already away fighting in the War) and more evacuees and neighbours. There was an impromptu party which went on late into the night, which staved off the time when people would realise the ramifications of what these young people would be doing, and what an uncertain future was ahead of them all!

Evan held his wife Sarah close that night, knowing that she was worried about Evan John flying, as was he. At least his beloved Sarah Kate would be reasonably safe working as a code and cipher officer. He must ask her, if it was at all possible, not to get involved with the Radar Stations (Radio Detection and Ranging) on the South Coast, it seemed that they were mostly in the line of fire! The only reason Evan was aware of these was because Joe Fleming had a colleague who had worked closely with this discovery, and apparently they could detect enemy aircraft by radio waves.

The next afternoon, when it was time for them to be driven to the Railway Station, for a few minutes Sarah Kate was in a quandary. She would really have loved to spend a bit more time with her family, but she also wanted to spend as much time with her twin as she could. Of course, she left with Evan John, after a tearful farewell from her parents and Megs.

The next evening Sarah walked towards the bar of The Royal Oak, Evan had said he would meet her there, but she had no intention of walking in by herself. How strange was she, unable to walk into a public house full of friends alone, yet with the training, hopefully, to defend her self in whatever circumstances might arise.

She need not have worried, as Jerome moved towards her from where he had been leaning against the ivy covered wall. His brown hair was ruffled, and his eyes enigmatic, and she felt a slight pain in her chest, which was not too painful, just unexpected. He stood on his cigarette to put it out and extended his hand towards her.

"Sarah Kate Evans, your brother will be just a little bit late. He is with one or two of his friends he hasn't seen for a while." He wasn't about to tell her that one of their colleagues who had learned to fly at the same time had gone 'missing' earlier in the day, and they had been waiting until long after he could possibly have turned up!

Sarah Kate put her hand in his, just to see if it had the same effect as previously. It did, only more so, and continued to tingle with awareness, as she was led towards The Royal Oak doorway. Once inside, Jerome dropped her hand, pulled out a chair for her, and then moved off to the bar, returning with their drinks.

Jerome sat down opposite to her, just as she noticed Evan John and Brian coming in through the doorway. He placed a piece of paper on the table pushing it across to her. "The address were I am living Sarah Kate, I want you to promise to get in touch with me if you need to for *any* reason. I am free tomorrow afternoon for a couple of hours, and so I'll see you outside here if you are free." He glanced at Brian and Evan. "You guys want the usual?"

Later Sarah felt frustrated, she did not get the opportunity to speak with Jerome alone, as a large group of pilots and their girlfriends put three tables together and had a very enjoyable evening, if a bit loud. However, by ten o'clock all the pilots were making their way home. Jerome had a car, and he insisted that Sarah should sit in the front seat, with Evan and Brian in the back. He dropped her off at the base, after managing to wind his left hand fingers through those on her right hand, and his squeeze made her heart-rate increase and she started to really look forward to tomorrow afternoon. From there she walked the short distance to the large country house where she now had a room, and realised it would be difficult to keep in touch with either Jerome or Evan John. It seemed strange checking in and checking out of the place that you were living!

That night she lay in bed wondering if Jerome was serious, or if there was any point in being serious anyway! People were moved about, and in very dangerous occupations, Jerome's and Evan's most of all. She sighed, she had been kissed by Dan and Zeke Williams at school, and had enjoyed being kissed on both cheeks by a French student at the university, who had eyes only for nicely rounded fellow students, and one other young man at university, but had found it all vaguely distasteful. However,

Jerome only had to squeeze her fingers, and she wanted more, and wanted him to kiss her like he had on the railway station platform before she had returned to Scotland. The things that had annoyed her about him, his voice, his attitude, his self-assurance now seemed to have the opposite effect on her. She should put her mind to all the training she had waded through in the last two months, as some time soon she would be expected to make good use of it! Instead of thinking what would happen if she met Jerome tomorrow, and should she even *consider* getting involved with anyone, least of all a Spitfire pilot, when she didn't even know where she was going to be for two days together? Her heart dropped, did what she had just thought also mean that Evan John should not get involved with someone, and get some happiness away from his flying?

Next morning it seemed that the time for her to act had come. She was awakened at six in the morning, and after a quick breakfast her briefing started and lasted all day. All day the conversations and instructions were given to her in French, and she was now expected to live the life of a young French woman, Violette Flamand. She was to be the younger sister of Jacques and Marianne Flamand, and deliver to the Resistance two wireless sets, and a very special suitcase. She was to help set up wireless communication with London, and she was to assist the Resistance in blowing up the fuel store of the occupying Germans in Verneuil, after which she would be picked up by a Lysander aircraft, or if things had not gone to plan she would make her way to the French Coast, and home to England. It all sounded very simple, or was she the simple one to even consider such a thing – as if she had any other option? They had not trained her so thoroughly just for her to walk away!

She was provided with clothing which had all been made in France, and it fitted her to perfection. She would have preferred something a bit more substantial. However, the cardigan and jacket were able to hide away her sleeve gun, and the obligatory knife she would have strapped to her thigh. She prayed that she would never have to use them. All these items were packed in her small suitcase, as she would be dropped into France in a jumpsuit, which would be buried along with her parachute. One of the group she had spoken French with all day, was of the opinion that at first any covert personnel had worn their uniforms, in case they were discovered and would be considered to be a spy without a uniform, but this had not been mentioned by anyone official.

It seemed that the Germans were advancing through the country with very little resistance, and were nearing Paris. North and slightly west of Paris was the River Oise, and she was to be dropped near the village of Sainte Pierre, and would be met by members of the French Resistance from that area, most of them living in and around the market town of Verneuil. She was asked to memorise a brief description of her 'brother and sister' Jacques and Marianne Flamand. Apparently Jacques had a useless arm, which was the reason he had not been called-up by the French forces, and he had been made to look older than his years, in order that the German's would not consider him worth sending to work in Germany for them!

Sarah was driven to an airstrip, and asked to wait in the armoured car, as someone would be coming to speak to her. She waited for over twenty minutes, and the time doing nothing made her start to wonder why she was there, and was it really what she wanted to do? She watched as another car drew up, and an RAF Officer slowly walked towards the car she was sitting in. He climbed into the car beside her, and she looked at him in surprise. It was the distinguished officer who had spoken to her in French, whom she had told that she wanted to learn to fly like her brother. She wondered if he remembered her, but was doubtful as she was wearing her jumpsuit, as she had been told it would be very cold on the flight, and the suit would be left in the aeroplane, or failing that buried with the parachutes.

He shuffled the papers he removed from his briefcase, and she noticed that one was a map, and she wondered if it would be given to her. Probably not, as if she was picked up it would be highly suspicious.

"Have they told you much about the aeroplane you will be flying in?" The Officer asked. He was very nicely spoken, his voice was low and somehow calming, and she realised she had only heard him speak French until now, except for a couple of words in English. She shook her head, and he continued, obviously trying to put her at her ease. "It is a very reliable little aeroplane, the Lysander, which is powered by a nine hundred horse power engine, affectionately known as the 'Lizzie' or 'The Flying Carrot' thanks to the shape of its fuselage. It is painted black, for the work it will be doing tonight, and the armaments have been taken away to allow for a reserve fuel tank to the fitted. There is a metal ladder fitted to the fuselage which will enable you to gain a quick entry or exit. They do a hundred and sixty five to two hundred and ten miles an hour, and only need a short take off and landing area." He paused, and Sarah began to think that he had not remembered *her* at all.

He put his hand onto his briefcase and picked up the map, and showed her the dropping zone, and she was pleased to have at least an idea of where she would be landing. She mentally noted the positions on the map of Verneuil, Sainte Pierre and the river Oise, and the dropping zone, and then handed back to him the map. Her one dread was that there might be nobody there to meet her, and if that dreadful thing happened, then she would at least know which direction to

29

take, she did have a compass, hidden on the back of her French wristwatch. He then drew a small envelope from his pocket, and opened it, looking very serious.

"This bit I don't like doing, and you will not have been told anything about this yet." He pulled out a pill from the envelope. "This is a Benzedrine pill, and it will keep you awake, if that should become necessary." He paused, and put the Benzedrine pill back in the envelope, and pulled out another pill. "There is only *one* 'L' tablet, in this little rubber cover, it is a suicide pill." He paused and glanced at her serious expression, "once bitten it will take only fifteen seconds. I trust that you will be able to *return them all* in due course." There was silence as Sarah Kate digested what had been said. She suddenly felt very cold, this wasn't just a very interesting and necessary adventure, and the task that had been set for her was deadly serious, with the accent on the 'dead.' She swallowed hard, thinking of Evan John.

"Is there anything you would like *me* to do for *you*," the Officer asked and put his hand over Sarah's cold one which rested on her knee, clutching the brown envelope, containing the hateful pills.

What on earth was she doing here, about to leave her twin, and also his friend Jerome? There seemed to be a connection between her and Jerome, and she hadn't had time to explore it! She also would have liked to talk with her parents and Megs. Was it too late for a change of mind, she wondered, staring at the officer beside her, and thinking of all her recent training, someone had to do this work and she had already been trained for it.

"There is something I should have done, but have not been allowed the time. I should have met someone this afternoon – Jerome Graham, he is a pilot at the RAF Station, and I would like him to know I'm sorry I couldn't make it." She gave the officer the address which he wrote in a notebook, and she was amazed that she had remembered the address, 13 Lime Street. "Also my brother, he is also my twin and a pilot, Evan John Evans. He may be a nuisance and look for me unless he is told I'm away again, and as I have been away for almost three months on and off, he will not be too surprised."

"It would be better if you wrote the notes. I will see they are delivered, keep it brief, and you do realise that I *will* read them both?" He tore two pages out of his note book and handed them to Sarah with his rather splendid fountain pen, giving her his notebook to lean on.

All she wrote to Jerome was, 'Sorry I couldn't make it,' and to Evan John 'I'll be away for a week or two brother. See you soon.'

She would have liked to say much more to both of them. Jerome's dark and knowledgeable eyes seemed to swim before her and she hoped they would meet once more. Evan was her twin and would understand what she felt, he always did.

The engine of a dark painted aeroplane started up, and the 'plane was slowly taxied onto the airstrip, and Sarah realised how small and insubstantial it appeared to be. The officer slowly moved out of the armoured car, and the driver got into it, and Sarah realised that all that she had to take into France must be in the boot of the car, and she was not being allowed to check it for herself. The officer bent down and looked in the back door towards her.

"You *are* going to fly my dear, but not quite as you wished. Bon chance Mademoiselle."

The fact that she now knew that he had remembered her, made her feel slightly better, at least one person knew who she was and where she was going! When she got time she would say a little prayer, not really for herself, but for her family who would be devastated if anything untoward happened to her, and for her twin, and also for the future that she was slightly worried about, as she wanted to *share* it with them!

When she entered the aeroplane she saw a man a few years older than her, he was already strapped into a parachute, and didn't even make eye contact with her. She imagined that he was either used to being parachuted into foreign countries, or he was petrified. She really hoped that he would be leaving the 'plane first, as she would feel better if there was nobody but herself and the dispatcher because she wasn't sure that she would not disgrace herself and panic.

CHAPTER FOUR

Jerome spent three hours outside The Royal Oak, and felt *almost* certain that if Sarah Kate could possibly have got away she would have. The first hour waiting seemed to drag, but having waited that long, he decided to wait, what else had he to do but wait and smoke too many cigarettes. His eager anticipation had soon turned to disappointment, and he started to wonder if he had been wrong about her character. He felt sure that she was 'untouched' and had not learned the strange wiles that some women resorted to in a relationship, or to trap a man. Evan was as straight as could be, and he had complete confidence in his sister Sarah Kate. Jerome *knew* he was right about her, but why wasn't she here - did she not *want* to meet him?

He had not come over to this country to get himself involved with a woman, but to help fight a War as he believed that Hitler should be stopped, and because he would be doing what he liked best, flying. However, although he had only seen her three times, she had gotten under his skin somehow, and he wasn't happy about what she appeared to be doing. It seemed too much of a coincidence that she spoke fluent French, and according to Evan quite good German! He nipped his cigarette between his fingers and flipped it away, shrugged his shoulders as he straightened up from leaning against the wall of the public house, and was surprised how very disappointed he felt.

Late in the evening he was stretched out on his bed, smoking again – his mother would be disappointed in him, she thought it was a disgusting habit. What was he thinking - he knew that his parents only wanted his safe return! He would have an early night and be up early in the morning, in time to have a word with Evan John, as perhaps *h*e would know the whereabouts of his sister! At their first meeting, he and Sarah Kate had seemed to strike sparks of each other almost as if they disliked each other, but he believed that had only been a way of dealing with their attraction.

There was a tap on the door, and he heard his landlady call out 'Note for you,' which was crumpled up as she pushed it under his bedroom door. He shot off the bed and picked it up, and straightened it out with his flat hands under the light on the dressing table. It was short and to the point.

'Sorry, I couldn't make it,' he read. It was signed 'Sarah Kate.' It looked as though the handwriting was usually very neat and tidy, but the 'Sarah Kate' seemed to have been written in a hurry. '*Couldn't* make it,' that meant that the note had been written *after* the two hours in the afternoon that she probably had meant to meet him! He was extremely disappointed, but also worried. Where had she gone off to this time, and how long would she be gone, as she had not known about this trip yesterday, of that he was certain?

Next morning, Jerome was watching the last rays of a spectacular sunrise, which gave the aircraft before him a pink tinge, when he was joined by Evan John. "It looks as though it will be a good clear day for flying," Jerome said by way of introduction. He was working up to asking Evan John if he had any objections if he started to date his sister.

"I have received a note from Sarah Kate this morning," Evan said staring ahead at the lines of aircraft on the apron. He now had Jerome's complete attention. "She said she would be away for a week or two."

"Well she has spent a lot of time away on courses, isn't that good news?" Jerome said, starting to light a cigarette.

"I don't know. I woke up with a feeling of foreboding, which didn't go away when I read the note. However, ..." Evan didn't get to finish his sentence as the siren screamed across the airfield. Jerome threw down his cigarette, and they set off at a run across the grass towards their aeroplanes. "Second to their 'plane buys the first beer tonight."

Jerome was taller than Evan John by about four inches, and he made it first, and they had nicely got the aeroplanes into the air and reasonably safe, when the first German planes could be heard, dodging flak from the guns surrounding the radar installations between the airfield and the coast. At the moment Jerome was fully occupied with the job in hand. Much later, when he wearily walked away from his plane, he wondered what Evan John had been about to say regarding his sister, as he was aware of the special affinity between the twins. Evan John would be just as tired as he was himself, so after a couple of drinks and something to eat, he would make a point of asking his friend about his sister!

CHAPTER FIVE

Sarah was aware that her last parachute jump from a static balloon should have been followed by a jump from an aircraft. For some reason they had not had time for the final jump, and she would very soon be rectifying that omission. The other passenger had already left the 'plane, without saying a word to either Sarah or the dispatcher. Now the dispatcher moved towards the centre of the 'plane, and lifted part of the floor of the fuselage away, revealing the hole in the floor. Sarah knew she must sit beside the hole in the floor, legs dangling ready to jump. The dispatcher hitched the static line of her parachute to a hook on the plane, and indicated the red light. She sat there with her legs dangling through the hole in the floor, and knew that when the light went green she must jump, ready or not, and she hoped she would be able to do it as silently as the previous passenger!

Just for a second she realised that the engines were cut to slow down the plane, and the green light came on and she jumped. She was free falling, and then her parachute opened, and she wanted to look up to see where the rest of her goods were following, but couldn't take her eyes off the ground below rushing towards her. It was almost dawn, and there was a bright glow showing in the east. She had a strange feeling of relief and euphoria, she glanced down, and the ground was there, coming nearer and nearer, she was down. She had just missed a small stand of trees, and the cool morning air was damp with a fine mist. She had landed on her feet and immediately she started to pull in her parachute as the air was so still. She had never felt so alive, and eager to complete her quest, and then return to her family.

She gathered up her parachute as quickly as possible, and grabbed the small shovel that was strapped to her leg. Where were the members of the Resistance who were supposed to meet her? Had she been off course? She looked around anxiously, and saw the two suitcases, and the wireless sets about thirty feet away. She must pull them underneath the nearby trees. She heard a sound behind and turned quickly with arms raised, ready to defend herself.

"Violette, what do you like to do?" a warm male voice asked urgently in French.

"I like shelling peas," she replied in his tongue. He nodded with relief, and took from her the small shovel, and indicated that she should help his colleague who was dragging the suitcases and wireless sets towards the trees. She had left her jump suit on the 'plane and she now felt quite cold, and she helped to bury the parachutes. She was amazed at how well Jacques worked, as his right arm was almost useless, it was thin and out of shape, and had been since his birth. Sarah had been warned about this defect, and also that his hair had been streaked with grey to make him appear older than his years. He wanted to stay with the Resistance and definitely not to be sent to Germany to work, and strived to appear a much older man.

Sarah and Jacques carried a suitcase each, and Marianne whom he quickly introduced as his sister, took the bag with the wireless sets, and they set off with a will towards the slowly rising sun.

For the next hour Sarah was thankful for the sensible lace-up shoes she wore with equally sensible socks. She was wearing both her cardigan and jacket and felt quite warm as they trudged along a narrow country road, just wide enough for a horse and cart or one small vehicle. Very little had been said between the three of them, and Sarah realised she had taken to speaking in French without much thought. She seemed to be coming down from her adrenalin 'high' and was feeling tired, and was relieved when they arrived at a barn, already almost filled with hay. A long ladder was placed against the stacked hay, and she watched as both Marianne and Jacques climbed up the ladder with their burdens. Jacques then indicated that she should climb up the ladder with her suitcase. She swallowed, and again speaking in French asked if he was going to remove the ladder, he nodded. She looked towards the barn door, and when Jacques would have stopped her moving over there, his sister Marianne stopped him and whispered to him. He nodded sagely, and Sarah Kate went outside to relieve herself before being, 'up the creek without a paddle,' or should that be 'in the hay without a ladder,' or maybe a 'bladder.' She stopped outside the barn and took a deep breath. Obviously, she was still a little high on either adrenaline or some sort of euphoria. She needed to calm down, and get her mind on her instructions, as tomorrow they would blow up the occupying Germans' ammunition store, that was why she was in this country!

Sarah had been instructed to only speak in French, and Jacques and Marianne were both relieved, as their English was not very good. Jacques informed her that there was food in the barn on the higher level, and she should make herself comfortable, as they would not be returning until a couple of hours before dusk the next day.

"We will remove the ladder and hide it before we leave. Is that *it*?" he indicated the suitcase that Sarah was carrying.

"Yes, this is *it*." She replied, and carefully climbed the ladder carrying the incendiary suitcase, and she glanced back and as the brother and sister started to move away, she suddenly felt very much alone.

When Jacques and Marianne had left, each on a bicycle, Sarah felt bereft, but started to take in her immediate surroundings. At least the night was not too dark and her eyes soon got used to it, and she began to see well enough to have something to eat. In fact she really enjoyed the French bread. She then fixed up one of the wireless sets with the light from her torch, ready for sending a message to London when the job was done, but she must not use the torch too much, or the wireless unless it was strictly necessary.

She made herself comfortable in her bed of hay, and tried to get to sleep. She thought of Evan, and prayed he was back at base safe and well. Then of Jerome, and wondered if he had received her note of regret, and had it meant anything to him, or was he out in The Royal Oak celebrating with the rest of his colleagues, and the women that seemed to be always there?

She had to get some sleep, but the shuffling and odd sounds of movement in the barn were keeping her awake. Bats or birds in the rafters did not bother her, but what was she sharing her bed with? She picked up the torch and shone it around, it shone on two pairs of beady staring eyes near her feet. She left the torch on, and put her hand into her suitcase. Yes, it was there, maybe it would do the trick. She could still see the shiny eyes of the rats, when she placed *her* rat which was almost twice as big just below her feet, and the tail was at least a foot in length. The shiny eyes disappeared in an instant, and she placed her rat carefully on top of her suitcase, maybe it would keep the others at bay long enough so that she could get some much needed sleep. She slipped into sleep still wondering why the 'exploding rat' had been packed in her suitcase, maybe it was to be used if they needed some sort of diversion, but the rats had moved away, did it smell, of rat or explosives? On the other hand her immediate senior in personnel knew that she would be living in a barn, what would be better than a rat! Her mind was too active, she must get some sleep.

Sarah awakened at five in the morning, when the sun came up and gradually burned away the mist. The hours until late afternoon seemed to drag. Two tiles on the roof had been moved slightly so that she could watch the surrounding countryside. All day she saw nothing, neither did she see Jacques and Marianne until they rode into the barn field making her heart jump, and then flood with relief. Minutes later Jacques placed the ladder against the haystack, and then moved away so that she could climb down.

From the corner of the barn Jacques unearthed another bicycle, with a large basket on the front, similar to the one on which Marianne had arrived at the barn. Sarah gazed at it with dismay, she could ride a bicycle, she had learned whilst delivering telegrams years ago just like her mother, but this one already looked rather heavy. They tied her incendiary suitcase into the basket, into which she also slipped the exploding rat. If anyone decided to investigate too closely they would get a big shock. They carefully placed hay to cover the suitcase and rat, and placed a number of summer greens and carrots on top. Jacques carried up into the barn the food that he had brought for her, and she wondered how much of it the rats might get before she managed to eat it! She grinned suddenly, what was she worrying about the last thing she felt like doing was eating at this particular time?

The ladder was taken down and laid on the floor of the barn, and Sarah Kate followed her colleagues outside, and was worried that Marianne was very attractive and that might mean that any German soldiers might remember her too easily. She placed a piece of straw where the door closed, hoping it would not have been disturbed before their return!

The plan was to cycle into Verneuil, have coffee in a small cafe and wait for the few German soldiers at the fuel store, to get drunk, or at least merry. This they had done every evening for the last fortnight since they had secured the town, on their way towards Paris. At this point 'Violette', Jacques and Marianne would plant the incendiary suitcase, which would cause the store to explode. Already it was quite natural for Jacques, Marianne and Violette to call each other by name.

It seemed a long ride to Verneuil without incident, and Sarah and Marianne settled in the cafe, and Jacques left the cafe for a moment and walked along the street with an older man quite short in stature who would not draw much attention, who Sarah realised was another member of the local Resistance group. She wondered how many people were in the group, and realised that she was unlikely to ever find out.

When Jacques returned at a leisurely pace, he confirmed that the store was stone built but the large doors were made of wood, and at the moment there was only one German soldier outside in the yard, and he was smoking and drinking wine. The older man with whom Jacques had walked along the street, now came and joined them at their table in front of the cafe. Jacques said quietly to Violette, "This is Jean Distelle, one of our colleagues."

Sarah nodded towards the older man, who had a small moustache, and had his short hair brushed severely back, but his eyes looked kind and he seemed quite excited.

41

"Did you notice the train pass a few minutes ago, behind the buildings over there?" Jean asked excitedly. They all nodded and he continued. "It was an ammunitions train, heading towards Paris. Another will pass in three days time."

"If we had known, we could have done something about it, instead of blowing up this ammunitions store." Jacques said with a disappointed sigh. "I know it will help to slow things down if we manage to do what we intend to this ammunitions store, but a train would be something else altogether."

"Is there another wooden door to this store?" Sarah asked, and received a nod from the older man, who looked at her closely with a keen interest.

"Just around the corner, from where that German soldier is sitting." He replied, with a quick glance across the quiet road.

"Out of his sight," she asked, and received a further nod.

"Is there anything flammable, like wood, straw or paper, which would *easily* ignite?" She asked, her mind racing and forming a plan that she thought they would disregard.

"There is the garage where they work on the vehicles, and yes there is a small wood store."

"If we started a big fire, which would then get to the ammunitions store, then we could do this job with the exploding rat. It might not be a complete success but it would cause a lot of problems for the Germans, and we could then use the incendiary suitcase to try and derail the train in three days time, and they just might think of today's problems as an accident. To derail the train would really slow down the German advance, and cause all sorts of problems."

"It's worth a try," Jacques said with a grin, and a nod. "The trains slow down to cross the bridge over the River Oise, and so that could be the best place to try. It could just work Violette, if you think there is enough explosive in that suitcase."

"There's not enough to blow up the carriages, but that could happen if we can derail the train somehow. We have three days to think about it." Sarah said broodingly.

"Let's try with the rat, and think about the rest later on. It will take a few minutes to get some wood and paper to start the fire." Jean Distelle decided, and looked a number of years younger in his excitement.

"I will activate the rat to explode in fifteen minutes. Can you get enough flammable material around it, place it between the garage and the wooden door to the ammunition store, and get back onto the road and far enough away in that time?" Sarah asked, trying to curb her building excitement.

"Yes we can," Jean said, "I'll carry the rat under my coat, Jacques and I will go together. Can you ladies start some sort of diversion, to keep the German soldier over there interested?"

Under cover of removing a few carrots and a couple of lettuce, Marianne collected the rat and slipped it onto the table covered by her headscarf, and Sarah pulled it towards the newspaper that was on the table.

Behind the newspaper, Sarah armed the rat, and handed it to the men under cover of the table, where it was slipped inside Jean's coat. They synchronized their watches, and the men moved off down the road.

Sarah wondered if Marianne was thinking what *she* was, that this was the longest fifteen minutes of her life! At fourteen minutes, Marianne stood up and shouted a mouthful of abuse at Violette and tipped her wine over her. Violette sprang up and in their 'girly' fight they knocked over the table, and kept up a tirade of abuse. With all this noise Sarah didn't actually hear the rat explode, but she did see a pall of smoke which gradually increased as it swirled around, and then she could see flames reaching above the building.

They heard a shrill cry of panic, "Herr Oberleutnant, kommen, kommen."

She whispered to Marianne "It's time to go. No doubt, Jacques will join us as soon as he can."

Without haste they moved to the bicycles still arguing and slowly made their way out of Verneuil. They had travelled half a mile when they heard the first big explosion, and minutes later Sarah began to worry that they had demolished half the town as they paused and looked back at the dark clouds of destruction over the town. Surely the local people would have been warned to keep away, was Sarah's first thought, and then she realised that to do that would have been very risky, and her thoughts dimmed the flush of success that she had been feeling.

Dusk fell very quickly, but there was a glow in the sky towards the town of Verneuil. They had to push their bikes in the darkness, and they were within half a mile of the barn when Jacques caught up with them. He was in high spirits, and Sarah had to calm him down by letting him know that she must contact London, and get permission to carry out the next part of their quickly thought out plan.

They approached the barn quietly and carefully, and the piece of straw that Sarah had left near the door handle was still there. Nobody had been inside the barn.

It was half an hour before they could contact London, and Sarah quickly found her code book, written in her own particular shorthand. She soon had a coded message ready to send. Jacques watched and listened avidly as she made contact with London. When she had finished he looked at her expectantly.

"We won't hear anything until tomorrow night. They will endeavour to check what we have told them, and then they will decide if we should try to derail the train. Something this big will cause a lot of repercussions, and they will want me to move on immediately. You should also make sure that you have covered your tracks, or move on out of town." Sarah looked at Jacques, who seemed really hyper, and she hoped he would not do anything rash. She had been amazed how well he managed everything with only one good arm. She would give him some responsibility, which might help to calm him down, and was important enough to fill his mind.

"I wonder if you could take away the spare wireless set, it is for the use of the Resistance, as is the one I am using. We should not have the two together as if I am found then they would get both wireless sets. You must be very careful Jacques, make sure that you, Marianne and the wireless are safe."

Sarah watched the brother and sister as they prepared to go back into the village of Sainte Pierre. They both had quite dark hair, but Marianne looked particularly pretty when she let her hair out of the plait which usually held her hair off her neck as it was pinned to the back of her head. Jacques looked much older than his years, because of the grey in his hair, and the strange way he held his damaged arm, but for the moment his eyes glowed with excitement.

"Can you come here tomorrow night, we might get an answer by then," Sarah Kate asked, wondering how she was going to get through the day with very little to keep her occupied. They agreed, climbed off the haystack, and removed the ladder.

Later she tried to settle down to sleep, after eating a meal of ham, cheese and bread, with a small glass of red wine, followed by water. She eventually settled in a sitting position, and was regretting that she did not have her trusty exploding rat to keep the real rats at a reasonable distance at least for a while.

The next morning she saw a farmer working in his field, he was a couple of fields away, and it did not seem that he would be a problem. She slipped out of the barn having slid down a rough wooden beam which came to within twelve feet of the rough floor. She desperately needed to attend to her personal needs, and she had seen a small stream just across the other side of the narrow road where she would be able to wash and the plane trees along the bank gave it some privacy. She did wash in the stream and it was bliss, and there was a foot bridge under which she could hide.

No sooner had she returned to the barn when she heard the sound of horse hooves on the narrow road, and literally dived into the hay and lay still. When the clip clop of the hooves had moved into the distance she came out of the hay covered in dust, and spent the next half hour trying to get her hair free of the dust with continual brushing.

Jacques and Marianne arrived to find Sarah ready to try to contact London. She was back on top of the hay, but had a few bruises received during her climb back, via the wall of the barn. Jacques and Marianne, of course, used the ladder!

Half an hour later, Jacques had to contain a whoop of joy when they received confirmation that they could attempt to derail the munitions train.

"Wait Jacques, it is not that simple, as we thought. They state that the incendiary suitcase alone is not powerful enough to derail the train. Some weakening, or undermining of the structure near the bridge will be necessary, and the only time that this can be done is after the train preceding the ammunitions train has passed through. They have contacted a Resistance group from another area, and they will meet Jean at the bridge, and the good news is that they too have an explosive devise, and the two together with a little undermining of the track should derail the train."

Jacques was making his way to his trusty bicycle. "That's not all Jacques, I will need papers to get me across France to the coast as a matter of urgency. Jean may be able to help us with that too. If we are successful the area will be full of Germans bent on revenge, I must disappear, and you must take great care." Sarah Kate was becoming worried that his excitement might make him careless, and she glanced at Marianne, who gave a little nod to Sarah Kate.

"Don't worry Violette, we will contact Jean as soon as possible about the necessary papers, and if we can't get them immediately you will have to stay with us in Sainte Pierre, as we might not be able to get food to you here in the barn, if the derailment is successful, as I know it will be." Marianne said with a confident grin.

Before following Jacques, Marianne gave Violette (Sarah Kate) a quick hug, and that human contact seemed to make them both feel much better!

CHAPTER SIX

Sarah knew from the coded message that she must leave the area immediately after the derailment attempt. After two such occurrences the Germans would be searching the whole area. They were unable to arrange for a Lysander to land anywhere nearby, as the Germans were on high alert, and she should make her way to the coast. Sarah had been briefed before leaving England in the Lysander, that at a convenient time they would arrange for her to be picked up by 'plane and returned to England. Because the fight between Marianne and Violette had been intended as a distraction at the Café in Verneuil, which had worked beautifully, now London had decided that 'Violette' could not stay in the area for any length of time, as the local people knew that Jacques and Marianne did not have a sister, and when the Germans came looking for revenge, it would not be safe for Violette to be in the area. She hoped that Jean would be able to help with the necessary paperwork, he didn't have much time!

The ride on bicycles from the outskirts of Sainte Pierre, which had of necessity to almost enter Verneuil to get to the railway bridge, was much more traumatic than the previous visit. Now the Germans would be aware of the possibility of other attempts to hold up their advance towards Paris, and onwards through France.

In a stand of trees overlooking the river Oise and the railway track, Jacques, Marianne and 'Violette' waited for Jean, and the waiting seemed interminable. The train preceding the ammunitions train, came and went without incident, and as soon as it had crossed over the river, men seemed to come from nowhere, and without anything being said except to Jean who arrived with them, they moved to undermine the railway bridge. Sarah Kate was worried about the necessary noise that resounded around the area, and then Jean indicated that she should follow him, which she did carrying the incendiary suitcase, which she duly armed, and handed it over to the man who appeared to be in charge of the Resistance group. Jean indicated that she should return to the stand of trees where Marianne was waiting with himself and Jacques.

Twenty minutes later Sarah was hiding amongst the trees on the hill overlooking the railway bridge. She was lying on her stomach in the thick grass, thinking that they should all be on their way back to St. Pierre before anything happened, there was absolutely nothing more that they could do here! Everything appeared to be in order, both Resistance groups had obviously worked together previously, and the undermining of the railway bridge and the fixing of the long pipe of explosives had been achieved without incident. Sarah had only ten minutes ago set the timer on the incendiary suitcase, and everyone prayed that the train would be on time, as was usual for the Germans, but not for the French!

Jean crawled towards her, complaining that he was too old for this, and with some difficulty because he was lying on his pocket, he pulled out an envelope.

49

"Violette, you are in luck. Your name is still Violette but no longer Flamand, it is now Marsaud. Here are your new papers, and good luck for your journey home. We will let other Resistance groups know that you are travelling north, and if you need help stick to your password 'shelling peas,' though how you will work that into the conversation I don't know." He left Sarah to peruse the paperwork, and took out a pair of binoculars which looked like opera glasses to Sarah, and surveyed the quiet country scene before him. She wondered if he was an opera fan when not at war! Sarah scanned the papers, and was surprised.

"Jean, these papers are authentic, how did you get them? Is Violette Marsaud likely to turn up at any time?" Sarah asked worriedly, and there was a long pause whilst Jean took a deep breath, and lowered his binoculars.

"Violette was the daughter of my cousin. Three weeks ago when the Germans over-ran this area, she was found in a wood, she had been er - molested by two German soldiers. Three days later she hanged herself in the same wood, she was waiting for her fiancé to return to marry her, and we can only guess that she thought he would not now want her. My cousin, Violette's mother, would like whoever assumes her identity, to do whatever she can to make things difficult for our enemies. You understand, her mother did not say 'difficult' or 'enemies.' She used much stronger words, and I'm still reeling from the shock." Jean said huskily. As he turned away from her he wiped his eyes. "As you can see from the photograph, you already have a look of the real Violette. I guess they taught you how to alter your appearance?"

"Yes Jean, they did. I guess I need to alter the parting in my hair, and plait my hair in the same style as Violette." Sarah said. She blinked away the tears as she thought of how desperate and violated Violette must have felt to end her own

50

life in such a horrible way. "I'm sorry Jean." Sarah said, and there was a loud explosion followed by a smaller one, which claimed their immediate attention. Damn, the train was just turning the corner to the bridge, there was the loud squeal of brakes, but it was too late as the weight of the train was carrying it forward to the bridge, and the first carriage nearly made it to the other side, but then there was a loud thud, followed by three loud explosions, as the first three carriages of ammunition exploded.

Sarah turned to see Jean being hugged by Jacques and Marianne briefly. Jean then kissed 'Violette' on both cheeks, and they all made their way to their various modes of transport. Jacques, Marianne and Sarah arrived at the barn two hours later, having been stopped once by an armoured car across the road, manned by two German soldiers.

Jacques had introduced his two sisters, Marianne and Violette Flamand, and Sarah had nearly died a thousand deaths as she realised the papers she had tucked into the bodice of her dress were in the name of Violette Marsaud! He told the soldiers that they were going to collect vegetables to sell in the small village of Sainte Pierre. For one dreadful moment when Jacques' back was turned, the younger of the two soldiers put his arm around Marianne and fumbled with her breast. Sarah saw the look on Marianne's face, and thought they were in deep, deep, trouble. However, Marianne whispered something in his ear, and the young soldier looked shocked and deeply embarrassed and got into the armoured car. Sarah felt a wave of relieve flood over her, if he had touched *her* breast he would have heard the rustle of paper. The second German looked at his colleague closely then followed, and they remained in the car, presumably waiting to interrogate the next people to come along the very quiet road, and the three bicycles moved along, desperately trying not to hurry.

As they rode along, with Marianne and Sarah abreast, and Jacques slightly behind, Sarah looked across at the other girl.

"What did you say to the younger soldier, I thought you were going to attack him where it hurts?"

"I said you and I liked to fondle *each other*, but Jacques might oblige him. Mind you Violette I didn't say *how* Jacques might oblige him," and she laughed out loud pleased that she had shocked yet another person. Marianne then made a stabbing movement, to show Sarah what she had really meant.

That evening only one word of code was transmitted to London *restitution*. From which they knew that the planned derailment had been a total success. Afterward, the wireless was taken to another place of safety by Jacques. That night he, his sister and Violette Flamand, spent the night in the village. Sarah said a tearful farewell to her 'brother and sister' and wondered if they would ever meet again, and at early light next morning, Violette *Marsaud* left the village having been given a lift by a local farmer to the next village, where she intended to catch a local bus travelling north.

Over the next three days Sarah was stopped a number of times to show her papers. But after the first time when her heart had been beating fit to burst, and she had put her hand through the torn pocket of her dress onto the knife tied to her thigh, just in case, she now felt more relaxed and it must have shown because she had no trouble in making her way to the coast. She felt desperately tired, having had very little sleep, because she kept hearing the squeal of brakes followed by loud explosions in her head, because she was finding it hard not to imagine the people manning the train, and wondering about their families.

She arrived at the fishing village suggested by Jean and Jacques, and went into a part of the port which smelled strongly of fish, and found some fishermen gutting fish.

"Can I buy some fish," she asked the older of the men, he paused for a moment with the knife raised, and then looked from side to side, then took in her dishevelled appearance and tired eyes.

"What do you like to eat with it, Mademoiselle?"

"Fresh peas, I like shelling peas," she replied.

The oldest of the men washed his hands, took her elbow and they walked through a door at the back of the shed, where she waited on a pile of sacking, and even had a little sleep. Later that night she was quietly welcomed onto a French fishing boat, where she felt relieved and even started to relax, thinking her long journey was nearly over.

Then began the most terrifying part of her adventure, crossing the English Channel, or as the French fishermen said 'La Manche.' No other shipping or aeroplanes seemed interested in the small fishing boat, but they still had to dodge everything that was offensively meant for both the English and the German shipping. Twice they were almost capsized by other large ships negotiating the Channel, and were often strafed by the German fighters returning home, during which time the crew and herself were thrown across the boat, and she lost a little time, and realised she must have been knocked out, as her head was throbbing as loud as the boat's engine. On top of all that the sea was particularly rough, and Sarah felt very ill when she was carefully manhandled from the French fishing boat, onto an English one mid Channel.

The next thing she could remember was waking up in a Police cell with a splitting headache and she crawled towards the door, but on hearing English being spoken, she crawled back to the bunk and went to sleep. Later in the day she was allowed to go to the washroom and clean herself up, and dress in some borrowed clothes, after she had managed to eat a sandwich and drink the best cup of tea she had ever received.

The next day a RAF vehicle arrived to pick her up, and the driver opened the back door for her. She climbed inside, and she was amazed to see the Wing Commander with the greying hair at his temples, who had seen her set off for France in the Lysander, it seemed to her that was weeks and weeks ago.

"How did you find me, I have felt so very ill since coming across the Channel, I think I must have had some sort of accident on the French fishing boat, my head has been very sore?"

He smiled briefly, and ordered the driver to proceed, and then he turned slightly in the seat next to her and smiled. "It seems our training up in the north of Scotland works. When asked who you were and who should be contacted, you gave the number that you had been given to memorise if you ever got in trouble with the local police, whilst out on your training runs, or mock operations. They, of course, contacted me, and here I am. Thank you for what you have done for your country, and after a thorough de-briefing, you will have two full weeks free to do as you wish. However, we don't want you to go home to your family just yet, it might look strange in the middle of a War, and it will be difficult for you to explain why you are home for so long, as you are not really injured."

"Thank you, I will be able to see my brother and colleagues?"

"Yes, of course. You will stay in your secure accommodation where you work, but you may see your RAF and WAAF colleagues. If you stay in the area you will also be able to go away for a few days, but somewhere we can contact you. Needless to stress, I hope, you will realise that you must not inform *anyone* where you have been or what you have been doing. Your de-briefing will start as soon as you awaken in the morning, whether it is 8 a.m. or 2 p.m. Have a good rest Sarah Kate Evans." The car stopped and he stepped out, and he gave her a slight wave, and she didn't know whether to wave or salute him! So she went to sleep as the driver put the car into gear and moved off, as it was the first time for days that she had felt really safe! One of her last thoughts before sleep claimed her was that she, thank goodness, would be able to return intact the small packet of pills that had been provided!

On the second day after her return she went to the RAF Base to see if she could contact Evan John, she was told that he should be back off operations in about three hours. She then asked about Jerome Graham, and was told that he had been flying on night operations, and should be at home sleeping, but he should not be disturbed!

Although she hadn't planned to, after an hour Sarah Kate went to 13 Lime Street, and asked Jerome's landlady Mrs Brown, if he was in. Mrs Brown was a friendly woman probably in her fifties, and she seemed younger, as she didn't seem the type to intrude in her lodgers lives, in fact the rules seemed to be non-existent. Mrs Brown was on her way out, and indicated the stairs. "Give a gentle knock dear, if he has had enough sleep he will probably hear you, and please shut the door behind you when you go out. Oh, you'll find Mr Graham, first door on the right, up two floors."

Sarah hesitated, it was too easy. Should it be that easy to get into someone's home, or had her recent training made her more suspicious of everyone she was to meet? She only wanted to apologise for being unable to meet him, was it three or four weeks ago – it felt like months.

She moved slowly and silently up the stairs as if she was on some undercover mission, but it felt really strange to be making her way upstairs towards a man's bedroom. If someone stopped her and asked what she was doing, what would she say – something in French probably!

She tapped gently on the door, twice, and whispered. "Jerome, it's Sarah Kate, I just wanted to apologise ..."

She got no further as the door was yanked open, and a bare arm shot out and grabbed her arm none too gently.

"I thought I was dreaming, and you would slip away." His voice was husky and he looked bemused. He was wearing nothing but a towel wrapped around his waist, he must sleep in the buff, and her heart thumped and she felt pink with embarrassment! She looked up into his expressive eyes, and felt she might drown in them.

"I will slip away, if you don't stop hurting my arm," she said, knowing how easily she could get him to let go, if she used her new found knowledge gained during her long training.

"Are you here to stay Sarah Kate?" He slowly let the pressure on her arm go.

"For a while Jerome, I'm sorry I couldn't meet you at the Royal Oak, and I hope you didn't wait very long." Sarah said breathlessly, and the pressure she had felt on her arm disappeared, and she didn't realise that he was wondering if he should admit that he had waited for three hours!

"Hell Sarah, can you wait whilst I go and take a bath and shave?" he asked. "I fell into bed the minute I got back after night operations."

"I've just arrived back here Jerome. I want to see Evan John when he gets in," she glanced at her watch. "He should be back in a couple of hours. You look alright to me Jerome."

He took her by the shoulders and pulled her into his room, and lowered her gently onto an upright chair. "You *will* see Evan John, sit there and don't move."

He grabbed a dressing gown from behind the door, and clutching his towel, he moved off down the corridor. He returned in four minutes wearing his dressing gown, and rubbing his fingers around his cheeks and chin, where he had obviously just shaved. She put her hand up to his chin without volition and felt how smooth it was, and he stopped suddenly. "Is it smooth enough to kiss you Sarah Kate?"

Her nod was hardly discernible, and his lips were on hers, and she clung to him until they had to breathe again. By now they were both lying on his bed, breathing hard.

"Sarah Kate you had better go and see your brother," Jerome said and tried to move away, but her hands held his shoulders. Her mind saw the photograph on the official papers of the deceased Violette Marsaud, and she thought of Violette's violent experience with the German soldiers, followed by an equally horrible death, at her own hand because she was unable to face her fiancé as she had been violated. Also how many young pilots had failed to return from operations, and some of them had been unable to experience so much that was good in life, which had been the same for her cousin Mary's husband Luke Williams. What if something happened to Jerome? All this flashed through her mind as if she was drowning.

"Jerome, I need you. Do you want to make love to me?" she pleaded earnestly, and he looked into her eyes and wondered what she had suffered, and knew it was not possible for him to deny her. They were both living on the edge, and anything could happen at any time! He had been starting to believe that he would never see her again, and yet she was here, now, and he believed that she wanted him, and he knew he would regret it for the rest of his life if he didn't

57

just for once behave in a reckless and selfish manner, and show Sarah Kate how much she meant to him!

"Is it me you need, and me you want to make love to you Sarah, are you really sure? Perhaps you only think this because of what you have been through recently?" he asked as he looked down into her beautiful, but tired, eyes.

"I've loved you since you first kissed me just before I left on the train, that weekend we first met, but I didn't realise it until I couldn't meet you at The Royal Oak," she admitted and thought he whispered 'me too' as his lips met hers.

Later they clung together covered only by a thin cotton sheet. All Sarah Kate could do was try to come down to earth, and she likened this experience to the euphoria that she had felt whilst parachute jumping, and then trebled it! She had never felt so happy, so fulfilled, or anxious to know that she had not disappointed him, being so inexperienced. Being so physically fit, she didn't feel any discomfort, in fact she wondered how soon – goodness she was a tramp! She looked into Jerome's disbelieving eyes, as he stared at her, and felt overwhelmed with love for him and only slightly shy as she tucked her face into his neck, as he held her tight.

Jerome held her close, this inexperienced beautiful girl from the north west hills had captivated him, he too had known this when she had not turned up to meet him at The Royal Oak, but after what had just happened between them, he knew that she was the only one for him, no other would do.

"Sarah Kate Evans, I'm in love with you, and after that glorious experience, I will have to marry you, you do realise that, and you will have to go to meet Evan John soon."

"Jerome, I would love to marry you, but I'm not quite sure, do you think we will ever be able to repeat something so blissful again?"

"Oh my lovely Sarah, I think we will," Jerome said with confidence laced with anticipation. They *were* very successful, and they *were* late for meeting Evan John, but then Evan John did not know that his sister had returned, until his Spitfire landed, and then he had needed to bathe, and rest for a while before going out.

When Evan John walked towards Sarah Kate and Jerome, he knew instantly that he had lost the exclusivity he had always felt with his twin, but he had gained a brother, something he had never had before, and his twin's choice could not be bettered. He was really happy for them, but he did just feel a little lonely. Now, he had to pretend to be surprised, and probably ask if Jerome's intentions were honourable. As if it mattered, at this time of war, when everyone lived from day to day, because it might just be their last! Since he had learned to fly and become a Spitfire pilot, Evan and Jerome had already lost five of their close friends. They should live for the day Evan thought, as there was no certainty about tomorrow.

CHAPTER SEVEN

Sarah Kate waited for Jerome to return to the table. She had been in The Royal Oak for half an hour now, with Evan John and Jerome. They had both moved off to the 'gents' and she assumed they were discussing her! Was she being paranoid or what? It was so difficult, she was not allowed to tell *anyone* what she did, or what she had been trained for. She knew that Evan John had a good idea what was going on, as she also believed that Jerome did too. She was worried that Jerome would try to stop her in some way, also that she would allow this, as she loved him so much she was frightened of losing him! She had always had a very close affinity with her twin, but now she also felt that she and Jerome were soul-mates. She was well aware, also, that her arriving back to the *big house* in the early hours of the morning would have been noticed, and 'C' as she thought of her Wing Commander, with the grey sideburns, and who spoke French like a native, would certainly have been informed.

Mrs Brown, Jerome's landlady, had proved to be surprisingly accommodating, she had not complained once about Sarah staying for most of the night with Jerome. Obviously she was on the side of true love, and Sarah and Jerome were also of the opinion that that was what they had. Jerome had asked for permission to marry from his Wing Commander, and when it was mentioned that he would be marrying a W.A.A.F, his CO could see no difficulties arising. Sarah could, and it really worried her. Sarah had a niggling worry, on the first day they had made love, no precautions had been taken. Jerome had later told her that he had not had any intention of getting involved with anyone whilst he was flying, that was the reason he had not been prepared, not because he was inconsiderate. Three weeks later she knew that she wasn't pregnant, and wasn't sure how she truly felt, she was just a bit disappointed. There would have been no way that 'C' would have sent her on a Lysander with a parachute with a belly large with child! Now she had Jerome she wasn't sure that she wanted that excitement again!

She knew that something would have to give, and it did, but it was not what she had imagined, but most certainly what she had dreaded.

It was mid August 1940, the newsreels and newspapers called it 'The Battle of Britain.' One thousand German planes were sent over Britain, and the RAF claimed to have destroyed six hundred and ninety four German 'planes, as against losing one hundred and fifty of their own. The RAF managed to save fifty seven of their pilots, they were irreplaceable, but the aeroplanes *were* replaceable given time. For pilots downed over the channel it was a torrid time if they survived the crash into the sea, as British Patrol Boats and German fighters *fought* to be the first to get to them.

Sarah was waiting at Jerome's lodgings, but he was a little late and she started to worry, and she joined Mrs Brown in the kitchen. At least there she would hear Jerome when he

61

came into the house. They talked of everything and everyone but of nothing important, and Sarah was really pleased to have company as she waited. He was very late, and Mrs Brown and Sarah had finished two pots of tea, when he at last arrived. Sarah heard his car, and met him at the door. She could tell immediately that something was wrong.

"What is it Jerome, what's wrong." He pulled her into his arms and held her tightly to him. He was so upset he could hardly get his words out.

"It's Evan John, his 'plane never returned this afternoon, in fact, *three* 'planes have not returned from our squadron. I have waited over two hours in case he had been hit, and was babying his 'plane home, but we've heard nothing, and his fuel will have been long gone. Evan and two of our colleagues have all been listed as missing. It doesn't look very hopeful, but don't give up entirely, he could still be alive. It all seems to be such bad luck, as we didn't have enough planes ready, at the beginning, and Evan was really upset because he thought he wasn't going to be able to fly!" Jerome sighed deeply, and held onto Sarah Kate, for his own comfort as well as for hers. "Do you want to tell your parents, or let the RAF do it?"

Sarah Kate moved slightly and noticed the dark patch of blue on Jerome's uniform jacket caused by her silent tears. She must pull herself together, as Jerome was as upset as was she as he and Evan John had been inseparable for months now.

"I'll tell them, we should go back to the Base, and then we will already be there if anything happens. I can tell your CO that initially I will inform our parents." She said quietly, all the time wishing she could scream and cry. Jerome looked as if he had been through more than enough for one day. She had been trained to school her emotions, now that training seemed to be paying off but at what cost!

"Sarah, what do you feel, you knew when I first met you that Evan had started flying and had a near miss. You sensed it."

"I know Jerome, but lately we have all had our ups and downs, I worry about you both. However, I haven't felt anything out of the ordinary today. It is really strange, you'd think that a 'plane crashing would set off some sort of reaction. Maybe it was very quick and he didn't suffer at all." Now she burst into tears, and Jerome knew it was the best thing that she could do, he had been very worried by her staunch resolve not to give in to her feelings. He held her close, and had to wipe his own eyes on the back of his hands, as she had his handkerchief.

When they returned to the RAF Base nothing further had been heard, and Sarah was shown into a small office, where she was given permission to ring home with the news that would devastate her family.

As soon as her mother answered the 'phone, and heard Sarah's voice, she was aware that her mother was expecting bad news.

"Is dad there," she asked, wondering which of her parents could bear the news best!

"Sarah Kate, it's dad, we love you. What's wrong?"

Sarah explained that Evan John had been listed as missing in action. She stressed the fact that he may have got his 'plane down safely, and she would let them know as soon as she heard anything at all.

"Is anyone there for you Sarah Kate, you should not be alone," Evan said his heart breaking for his daughter who had probably lost her twin brother.

"I have a friend of Evan's, a pilot, who is staying with me until we hear something definite. I love you dad, and you mam, please look after Megs, she is so proud of Evan John." She put the 'phone down, and rested her head on the desk,

63

they would all be helping each other, as usual, the whole family would pull together. She remembered the hero worship that the evacuees Bernard and Brenda Maitland had shown towards Evan John, now there were two extra hearts to be wrenched by this news. She couldn't bear thinking about her Great Grandma Kate who had already lost family members, and now possibly one of her grandsons, she always put on such a brave face for the family but Sarah Kate knew she sobbed inwardly.

Two days later Jerome and Sarah were granted permission to marry by special licence, and this was arranged to take place in a further two days. There was no news of Evan John, and Sarah was getting more nervous every day that Jerome had to fly. The best way for her to get through the days was to get on with her work as a Code and Cipher Officer, which she undertook in the *big house*, where she now lived. At first Jerome had wanted to know where she lived, but accepted the fact that she was not able to tell him. He now worried more than ever about her, and was relieved that she still had a couple of days left of her 'repatriation holiday' which was what Jerome now believed it to be, and this would encompass the wedding. She had told Jerome that she was heartbreakingly bereft, without her twin, and she needed to become one with him more than ever.

Sarah Kate decided to get married in her WAAF uniform, and mourned the parachute silk which she knew to be buried in a wood near Sainte Pierre! Which, of course, got her thinking of Jacques and Marianne Flamand, and the more mature Jean Distelle, and she couldn't discuss those feelings with anyone! How terrible it was to be living under German Occupation. Surely they would never be allowed to cross the English Channel, except in 'planes which were thankfully picked up on the new secret Radar (Radio Direction and

Range). Secret except to the RAF, which gave the British air crew advance warning, and therefore, a slight advantage.

Sarah dressed for her Wedding with care, and wondered if they should be going ahead with it, as nothing had been heard about the missing airmen. She was to meet Jerome at the Registry Office, and she was pleased that Mrs Brown had agreed to accompany her. They went inside just as the previous wedding party came out, and the groom was in uniform, and the whole party were loud and excited. Sarah nodded to the young couple, and started to wonder if Jerome was coming, had he changed his mind, and she had always believed that whenever she got married, then her twin would be there beside her. A rogue tear ran down her cheek and Mrs Brown put a comforting arm around her shoulders.

Sarah almost collapsed when she stared in disbelief at the figure of Evan John struggling towards her on crutches, with his leg in plaster, and a large bandage around his injured head. He staggered back as she rushed towards him, "Don't touch me Sarah Kate, I'm in pain." She hugged him until he winced with pain, and then berated him for not letting her know he was alive, as she gently touched the bandage around his head.

"I couldn't, somehow I managed to get out of the 'plane in the English Channel, and saw a fishing boat nearby, in fact I tried to ditch as near to it as possible, they must have dragged me into their boat and brought me ashore, and then to hospital. I lost my dog-tag, and until I came around nobody knew who I was, and all the time German planes were firing at us. Your husband to be is parking his car, now he has managed to recover from the shock of seeing me. Oh he's here now."

Sarah very nearly said *she knew* how that felt to be in the English Channel, instead she took Jerome's waiting arm, and walked into the Registry Office, with the groans and thumps of her brother following, and the sound was music to her ears! Her twin brother was here safe, if not well, and she was marrying the man she loved, she was so very happy!

She turned back just before the wedding service. "Evan John, have you told our parents?"

"Yes, I spoke to them on the 'phone earlier. I didn't say you were getting married because I didn't know until I found Jerome."

"Good, I guess mam, dad and Megs might be glad, but the rest of the family would not understand how I could do that when you were missing. Don't tell them, I don't want them upset."

"Could we get on with this service please, I have another in twenty minutes," the Registrar said kindly, not wanting to stop this very interesting conversation, but needs must! Sarah Kate wondered absently what they would have done without two witnesses, because if Evan John had not returned then they would only have had Mrs Brown, they would probably have had to drag someone off the street.

Sarah thought of her mother's wedding at Gretna Green which had been much talked about, and now she was also to be married by a Registrar, she hoped that her sister Megs would manage to do a better job in due course. She was so very happy to be marrying Jerome, and so very happy that Evan John had returned safe and almost well - then why was she unable to stop crying?

Sarah Kate had been granted a further three days off, which she thought was because of the return of Evan John. However, Evan John insisted that they should take a cottage in South Wales, which had been offered to them, and at least have a three day honeymoon, after such a frugal Wedding. Evan John was to travel to the Lake District to have time with his family to recuperate, and when he was well enough he was to return to take up a desk job for the time being.

The only downside to Evan John's return was that the other too airmen missing, had *not* returned. This was brought home to them when they listened to Winston Churchill's exuberant and confident pep talk to the nation on the BBC wireless in which he mentioned the Battle of Britain in the Air, saying in his distinctive voice, "Never in the field of human conflict was so much owed by so many to so few."

Sarah could not remember much about Wales. However, she and Jerome talked, made love, and talked again until they really knew each other's pasts, likes, dislikes and plans for the future, which of course, had to be put on hold – there was a war in progress, and they were both a part of it.

Sarah Kate spent her evenings and nights at 13 Lime Street with Jerome, and worked at the *big house* during the days. She had spoken with 'C' and they had agreed that for the moment at least, Sarah was a Code and Cipher Officer, but 'C' had not let her off the hook altogether. He had been really appreciative of what she and the Resistance group had managed, particularly as the spectacular derailment had been their idea in the first place, and a bonus as regards her mission. The loss of the vast amount of ammunition from that munitions train had slowed down the German advance towards Paris considerably.

Another blow was to hit the Birkett and Evans families, in fact it was a double-whammy! Evan and Sarah's maternal Uncle Matthew had been killed whilst fighting with the Border Regiment, devastating his wife Megan (who was also their dad's sister). Sarah Kate and Evan John were advised that the whole valley were pulling together to help Megan get through her dreadful loss, when the matriarch of the family, Great Grandma Kate Birkett, found all this too much to bear and slipped away during her sleep. There was nobody in the valley who could remember a time without the estimable Kate Birkett. Sarah Kate and Evan John were unable to get leave to see their great grandmother laid to rest, and said a private goodbye in their prayers.

Sarah Kate talked at length with Jerome about the valley and her family, and told him of how her great grandmother managed to embrace the old with new when it came to either language or just village life, and some of her old sayings which were still pertinent today.

Sometimes Sarah Kate seemed a little left out when Evan John and Jerome talked of their days of flying, which were not getting any shorter or less hazardous for Jerome. However, Evan John was chomping at the bit, as he had not yet been allowed to go back to flying. He desperately wanted to fly again, but had a sneaking feeling that he might have used up his luck. When he did start again a few weeks later, he said it was like riding a bike, you didn't forget how to do it! Sarah also wanted to be more involved - she didn't really want to go back to being a Special Operations Executive, did she?

In September it was reported in the newspapers that three hundred German bombers escorted by double the number of fighters had flown up the Thames. They bombed a power station, Woolwich arsenal, a gas works, the docks and the city. Two hours later more bombers arrived. The French spoke of London as an 'ocean of flames,' but still London managed to carry on with its daily life. Again Sarah began to think that she should be more involved, she had been trained to be so much more than a Code and Cipher Officer. However, she did wonder if she might be pregnant although precautions had been taken, and there was nothing she wanted more than Jerome's child, if a mistake had been made then it was the will of God or just kismet!

Late one afternoon when Sarah was thinking of packing up work, and leaving for 13 Lime Street, 'C' called by her desk, and she was surprised when he sat down opposite her.

"I think you should go to the RAF Base, there has been a nasty dog-fight over the channel, and a number of planes have failed to return. Your husband and your brother have not yet flown in. As the planes arrive back the pilots are being de-briefed for information. Good Luck." He watched as she tidied her desk, and put on her uniform jacket, and quietly left the room. She could well be one of his very *best* operatives, as she had kept her emotions well under control. He really admired her, and hoped that she would come back with good news, as she looked very lonely as she walked away from him, with only a slight stoop to her shoulders!

Sarah walked away from 'C' determined not to believe the worst. Evan John had returned bloodied but whole after a dunking in the sea, and she hadn't felt any strange pangs. As for Jerome, he didn't need to be fighting, he was Canadian and had volunteered, and he should be at home with his family, damn him. If that were the case then she would never had known and loved him! She felt like curling up like a ball and hiding away, but she needed to know what had taken place on this terrible day. She would cry later, whatever happened.

Evan John was one of the last to arrive back. His plane had suffered considerable damage but he managed to bring it down where it belly-flopped. However, he had been using up as much fuel as possible, and the fire engine was there immediately, and Evan John was hauled out and put into an ambulance. However, when the ambulance stopped he walked away from it, and headed towards his sister.

"Jerome, is he back?" But he was aware from Sarah's drawn face that he was not, and his chest ached for her.

Evan took her hand and never let it go, as they sat down to wait. They waited until an Officer came to tell them the results of the de-briefing of the pilots.

There had been three different sightings of Jerome's plane, which was on fire, and although he appeared to have some sort of control he was making for the sea. There were two sightings of his plane, which looked like a ball of fire, disappearing towards a forest, near the French coast.

"Your husband was a wonderful man, Mrs Graham, he came to us from Canada as an experienced pilot, and he was a great help advising the younger pilots, like your brother here. He will be sadly missed." He paused and looked slightly embarrassed. "We have your husband's parents down as next of kin, so we will have to inform them."

"If you would Sir, thank you. I will be going through my husbands things, and will then contact them." Sarah said woodenly. She didn't like to admit that she did not have her in-law's address, they had been married for only two months, and she assumed there would never be any busier months in the future! She wished everyone would leave her alone, except Evan John of course, she would need him for a couple of days, and then she must get her life into some sort of order. It would not be right if she didn't do something to make Jerome's death mean something - she would carry on the fight he had started, if she could even *exist* without him! Suddenly her legs gave way beneath her, it wasn't fair, the love of her life had gone, and she was really doubtful that she could live and function without him!

Before they left the RAF base, the officer returned to them with the news that a spitfire had been seen from the air, or the remains of it, a few miles from the French coast. There was no sign of a body, but the plane had exploded, whether on impact or later they could not tell.

70

Evan escorted his sister to 13 Lime Street, where she talked for over an hour to an inconsolable Mrs Brown. She decided she could not possibly sleep upstairs, and after agreeing that Mrs Brown should pack up Jerome's things, she asked Evan to take her to the *big house*. For once she had not thought to keep where she was living to herself. Evan realised this, and did not bother her, she would probably have forgotten her lapse by morning.

When she awoke in the morning after having only two hours sleep, she thought of the hours she had been awake dry eyed unable to cry. Now she cried, as if she would never stop. The hope that she might be pregnant was now gone forever, what was there for her to live for? Nothing! Except extracting some sort of vengeance from the enemy on behalf of her family, both the living and the dead. The dead being her cousin Mary's husband, Luke Williams, her Uncle Matthew and now her husband Jerome. She felt very low, and wondered if she could carry on without Jerome, her heart was like a lead weight, but what else could she do? She thanked her Guardian Angel for giving her the short but blissful time she had spent with Jerome - but if he was so damned clever, why hadn't he *saved* Jerome!

Her mind was in turmoil, and she realised that she should take stock of her position, think everything through carefully, and then decide what to do with her life. Thank God for Evan John, he too had loved Jerome, as a new member of the family and his friend, and he would be there for her over the coming months and years, just as she would be there for him. The wonderful time she had enjoyed together with her husband had been way to short!

CHAPTER EIGHT

Sarah requested an interview with 'C' and was granted one immediately. He was pleased that she wanted to return to being a Special Operations Executive, but he insisted that she undertook a psychological assessment, having gone through the trauma of her husband and brother going missing, and finally the death of her husband. At first Sarah was really annoyed, she had expected to be welcomed back immediately, but later realised that she could possibly want to go back to that hard and dangerous life, for the wrong reasons.

The psychological assessment was quickly arranged, and she answered all their questions as best she could. Believing all the while that there was no way they would turn her down. She knew that they had not put her through all that training to turn her away. Besides all that, would they *care* if she didn't return as long as she performed the tasks allotted to her, and provided them with the information they sought? Afterwards she thought she was being very cynical. At the moment she felt bereft, but she knew that she *did want* to return to see her twin again, and to be welcomed back into the bosom of her family. Also her CO would want her to return, if only to send her back at some later date! Perhaps she would be able, with her fellow covert operators if only in a small way, to help to bring this war to an end! Two and a half years and the 'six month War' was still ongoing!

Her return could not have been timed better. Verneuil being only a matter of seventy odd miles from Paris was used as a dormitory town for the German Officers, and the Chateau Genevieve on the outskirts of the town had been requisitioned by the Army of Occupation. Once again, Violette Marsaud was a perfect cover for Sarah as her papers were authentic, and the death of the young woman by her own hand had been hushed up by her family, so that her identity could be used, with the blessing of the real Violette's mother. Violette was to be parachuted in as before, from a Lysander aircraft. She was to take with her various items for the Resistance, and she was to join the *real* Violette Marsaud's cousin, in Verneuil. He was forty seven years old, and ran a Cafe and Bakery, and had always lived there, his name was Gerrard Marsaud. His cousin, Violette Marsaud (Sarah Kate) was the product of a late marriage by his father's brother.

Violette had to bring in some incendiary devices, together with two more wireless sets, as one had been destroyed in terrible circumstances. This terrible occurrence had been reported to London by Jean Distelle himself. One of the wireless sets had been found in the home of Monsieur Distelle senior, during a random search by the German SS, Jean had not been around and luckily neither had his mother, and because Jean's father would not say anything, he had been shot and the wireless destroyed. Jean had then taken his eighty year old mother to live with her cousin outside Sainte Pierre in a farming area. Jean's mother's cousin was, of course, the mother of the deceased Violette Marsaud, and

Jean was now keeping away from Sainte Pierre as much as possible and, in fact, he was keeping a very low profile.

Violette's mission was to get any information gleaned from the German officers in the chateau, either from the reluctant staff, or vigilant observers, and pass this on by coded wireless messages to London. Sometimes even a snippet of conversation gave away to the experts in London an idea of the German's intentions, when put together with other snippets. There were a few local girls who were frequently asked to the Chateau for a meal, a drink and to dance. Most were worried about their families, and went against their will, but all were anxious to help the Resistance and the enemies of the Third Reich.

Oberst (Colonel) Werner Muller, the Commander at the Chateau Genevieve, had promised the Mayor of Verneuil that these young ladies would come to no harm, and that promise had been kept. This did not mean that should any young lady succumb to temptation she would be banned from the Chateau! Nor was there anything to stop them being reviled by the local population, for doing anything more than *visit* the Chateau! Most of them only agreed to attend the Chateau to keep their families safe from an ever present threat of violence by the army of occupation.

During the afternoon that Sarah was to be dropped into France after dusk, she went to say goodbye to her brother. He wanted to dissuade her from any further action, particularly as he had no idea where she would be, and how dangerous it might be for her. However, he looked into her determined face, and knew that nothing he could say would deter her. Many times in the last few days she had mentioned the death of their Uncle Matthew and Luke Williams from their home village. She was also aware that their cousins Harold Benjamin and Johnny Birkett were away fighting with the Border Regiment, together with their Uncle Charlie

Jones, and a neighbour Zeke Williams who had enlisted after the death of his younger brother, Luke.

He kissed her on both cheeks, and she seemed quite cheerful, but resigned, as she left him at the RAF base. He shook his head in dismay - was there anything he could have said that would have made a difference and made her stay? He had noticed that she never mentioned Jerome, and he had been worried when Mrs Brown had met him outside the Royal Oak one afternoon whilst out shopping, and she had mentioned that Sarah Kate had not yet been to collect her husband's belongings. It was as though Sarah Kate couldn't accept what had happened to Jerome, and Evan John thought he understood how she must be feeling, if anything happened to Sarah Kate, his twin, it would be as though part of him had died.

****

Sarah waited already in her jumpsuit, with everything packed in the boot of the car ready to be transferred to the Lysander ready for take off, and wondered if 'C' her Wing Commander would arrive, or would it be someone else? She stared straight ahead as she waited in the vehicle. She could see Jerome's beloved face in front of her superimposed over the air strip and black painted Lysander in front of her. How she loved him, and how little time they had spent together. She would have to deal with his belongings and get in touch with his parents in due course. For now, it was just too painful and heart-wrenching. She stared ahead and could still see his eyes and the love they had always shown her. It was only seven days since he had been killed, and she could see him clearly, but how long would it be before she couldn't remember him? Is that what happened when someone died and left loved ones behind? She wiped a tear from her eye, just in time, as her CO opened the car door and sat down beside her.

"Are you sure about this Private Evans, er Graham?" He asked, and she nodded, still a bit emotional from her thoughts, but determined not to show him how she felt.

He showed her the map of the drop zone, which was almost the same as the last time. He then handed the envelope with the pills to keep her awake, and the suicide pill. "Bring those pills back to me again please, and take care. Bon chance."

He vacated the car and saluted her, which she returned in surprise. She was not dressed correctly to be saluting a senior officer, and he seemed to be in a hurry. The last time she had left he had said "Bon chance Mademoiselle." Perhaps he thought he had been kind not to use her new title, Madame, which was presumably the same for a widow!

The driver set the car in motion, and Sarah looked out of the back window, and saw another car arrive beside the CO screeching to a sudden stop, and the driver slipped out from behind the wheel waving his arms excitedly. Something interesting had definitely occurred. Her Wing Commander seemed to reprimand the man for this interruption, but listened intently to what he had to say. He turned and gave Sarah a slow wave as she climbed up the metal steps into the fuselage. All too soon the Lysander was gathering speed along the runway, into the unknown, but this time Sarah Kate had at least a good idea of what was expected of her.

The Wing Commander stood watching as the small 'plane disappeared into the distance. He had just made a life-changing decision in the course of just a few seconds. He had not got to this stage in his career without having to make important life changing decisions, as a matter of course. However, it was not *his* life that might change, and this did not make him feel even the tiniest bit better, or even like himself! He was the pits, and so was his job! He doubted if he would get much sleep tonight!

After an uneventful flight in which Sarah was the only passenger and a stilted conversation with the dispatcher, in a small wood near to the village of Sainte Pierre, France, two parachutes slowly sank to the ground. As the night was moon lit, Sarah quickly gathered up her parachute, and turned to collect the parachute from the supplies which had dropped nearby. She dragged everything towards the area under the trees where it was quite dark, and crouched down to listen. Where were Jean Distelle or Jacques and Marianne Flamand? She couldn't hear anything, but could see a light moving towards Sainte Pierre, and then she heard the sound of a motorcycle, or motorcycle and sidecar. It must be a motorcycle and sidecar as a light shone first on one side of the road then the other, as the vehicle slowly made its way towards St. Pierre. As it passed near to the wooded area, Sarah heard voices speaking in German. She started to worry, what had happened to the Resistance members who should have met her. It was moonlight, but could she remember the way they had taken to the barn the last time? Even if she did, she could not carry the incendiary devices and the wireless sets as well as her few belongings.

She quickly took the spade strapped to her thigh and started to bury the parachutes. She was very hot and quite dirty by the time she had finished. She looked around her in the moonlight.

It seemed that at some time the fields had been cleared of large rocks and these had been put amongst the trees, or even placed there before the trees had grown. She managed to move some of them and made a hiding place for the things she couldn't carry, and hid any signs of disturbance with last years dry leaves and twigs. She noticed that already the leaves were changing to autumn colours, and some were already falling. Well the French autumn, according to tonight was quite calm and balmy, and she hoped she would be back

77

in England before the onslaught of winter – maybe it was quite mild in France.

Where were the members of the Resistance, it must be an hour or so since she had been parachuted in? In a way she was pleased with the moonlight, at least she recognised the area, if it had been dark she would probably have thought she had been dropped in the wrong zone!

She swung herself up into a plane tree on the outskirts of the wood, hoping to see through the leaves to survey the area. Once more a vehicle went passed with a light swinging from side to side. The area appeared to be monitored by the occupying Germans much more than when it had first been captured on her last visit, and very likely she and the Resistance were the reason for that! She would have to move before daylight, but she would wait a while and hope that the clouds just to the north would move over the brilliant moon. Sarah remembered that in the middle of June last, from the BBC in London De Gaulle had urged the French to 'Fight on,' and since then in July the French had signed an armistice with the Germans, and the German terms had been merciless. It looked as if the armistice had not changed anything, judging by the number of German Patrols even in the rural areas.

She clutched the branch tightly trying not to dislodge any leaves as there was something *moving* below. It might be a rabbit or something, whatever lives in the countryside in France! If it was the Resistance she had not heard them approaching!

"Violette," a whisper hung in the air in strongly accented French. "How do you prepare your vegetables?"

Sarah gave a sigh of relief it was either Jean or Jacques.

"I like shelling peas," Sarah said with relief in French, and dropped silently down out of the tree causing Jean to clutch at his chest in shock.

Even in the moonlight streaking through the tree branches Sarah could tell that Jean had aged since they last met. He looked like an old man, but he had suffered the loss of his father in terrible circumstances.

"Where is Jacques?"

"Recovering from getting beaten up by the German SS who shot my father, he tried to help him. Enough Violette, we must get moving. Where are the goods you brought in with you?" Jean said in a very businesslike manner, he waved an arm and Marianne joined them and gave Violette a quick hug, and Sarah felt just a little better about the whole business, she *was* remembered and it seemed, welcome.

"I hid everything over here," Sarah said moving to the area of piled up stones.

"Well done Violette. We will take only one wireless set, which Marianne can carry, I will take one of the incendiary devices, Violette, you must carry your own belongings. The rest we will get later. We must move quickly."

"Where are you taking me," Violette asked setting her pace to match that of Jean. Marianne was already ahead.

"To Sainte Pierre, but just for tonight, tomorrow you will go by bus into Verneuil to Cafe Marsaud, to meet again your cousin Gerrard. Monsieur Gerrard Marsaud will make you welcome, he hasn't seen you for a number of years, if anyone asks. Monsieur Marsaud will have a sticking plaster on his elbow, just so you will know which man is your 'cousin,' as the Cafe and Bakery are usually quite busy." Jean said breathlessly, and Sarah slowed her pace.

"That seems straight forward. How do I contact you Jean, and where will the wireless be for contacting London."

"For the moment the wireless will be with you, but it will not be safe to use except very occasionally from the Cafe. I will let you know. Violette, your 'mother' is also a cousin of mine, but I don't want that mentioned in the Cafe not after

79

what happened to my father, so Monsieur Marsaud will only acknowledge me as a customer. Any message I have for you will be handed to you with money to pay for the bread buns I shall buy from you, any message from you will be inside one of the buns."

They paused at the outskirts of Sainte Pierre, whilst Marianne disappeared for a few minutes, obviously to hide away the wireless set, as she didn't have it a few minutes later when she returned. Jean left them, and Marianne took Sarah into her home, and showed her the living room where she could sleep on a small sofa, until the morning. Sarah managed a few hours sleep as a necessity, and when she moved into the kitchen the next morning she was very worried.

"Marianne, where is the wireless?" She asked abruptly.

"I have fixed it into a bicycle basket, and it has been covered by vegetables," Marianne smiled briefly, "without an exploding rat. I will ride into Verneuil tomorrow afternoon, delivering some vegetables to the Bakery. People know me, and won't ask any questions. You, however, will be quite new on the bus and you may be questioned. However, you will have all the necessary paperwork, and will have your 'cousin' to vouch for you, when you arrive in Verneuil."

Later Sarah looked in the small mirror in Marianne's kitchen, turned this way and that, and was quite pleased with the likeness to the photograph on the identity papers which had belonged to the unfortunate Mademoiselle Violette Marsaud. She looked quite pretty, and was determined that she would not suffer the turmoil and despondency of the younger girl! She turned as the door opened, and was relieved when Jacques entered the room silently, but he placed a hand to his heart in surprise.

"My God Violette, I thought you had come back from the dead," Jacques said and quickly sat down at the kitchen table after breathing deeply.

Sarah was equally shocked, as Jacques looked terrible, and was obviously still suffering from the beating he had received at the hands of the German SS, when he had tried to intervene between them and Jean's father, Monsieur Distelle. Notwithstanding his wizened arm, Jacques looked really ill, and looked as if all the life had been beaten out of him. No wonder he had not accompanied his sister and Jean last night. She kissed him on both cheeks before collecting her bags and putting on her thick coat ready to move to the bus stop. Poor Jacques, had he ever had the luck that she had – the total delight in loving someone to distraction, being loved in return, and wonderful memories to run through her overactive mind. Sometimes she thought she could almost touch Jerome her feelings were so strong, and those strong feelings made her feel that he was beside her. And yes, she *could* still see his handsome loving face in her minds eye.

Sarah shook her head. It was hard to believe that it was only nine hours since she had left England, every minute had been packed with some emotion, which proved to her that she was still alive, even without Jerome, and as she was alive, she might as well do something useful for her brother, her family, and her country.

CHAPTER NINE

Evan John climbed wearily out of his Spitfire, he had been escorting bombers, and he needed a bath and a long drink in that order. It had been another shattering day, he was so tired, and so worried. He was sure Brian had bought it today, his plane had taken a direct hit, and he had watched it disappear through the clouds below into probable oblivion. Evan walked slowly into the building and looked at the faces of his colleagues who had landed before him. It was not good news.

He would think about Brian, his family and friends later, for the moment his mind was on Sarah Kate. He had a sinking feeling that everything was not well, but could not explain his feelings. He would ring Rowan Trees later, just on the off-chance that Sarah Kate had decided to have a word with their parents and Megs. The one thing she would not have done was to tell them what she was doing, and where she was doing it! He walked into the Wing Commander's office, where the pilots would be debriefed after the day's flying, and the Wing Commander looked up and saw it was Evan John, and indicated the chair opposite.

Evan John sat down with relief, and looked hard at his Wing Commander when his batman brought two cups of tea and placed one before the Wing Commander and one before Evan, which was unheard of. His heart dropped into his boots, what else could go wrong today!

"I'd drink that down if I were you," the Wing Commander said brusquely.

Evan did, and hoped he was going to be able to keep it down.

"It's really *good* news Evans. At about eighteen hundred hours yesterday we heard that a John Doe had been brought into the hospital a few days earlier, suffering with burns and concussion, and he might possibly be air crew, but was wearing rural French clothing, we don't know how he came across the channel, and he did not have a dog-tag. Today he started to remember, and says that he is Jerome Graham a pilot, and is demanding to see his wife."

Evan stared across the desk with stunned incredulity, and then looked ecstatic, and then his heart dropped. Would it be possible to contact Sarah Kate after visiting the hospital to ascertain that it was indeed Jerome?

"I've taken the liberty of ordering a car and driver to take you through to the hospital, to ascertain whether or not your brother-in-law has survived. It will be outside in about an hour, which should give you time to get cleaned up and something to eat. You *will* ring me and confirm things either way as soon as possible." His Wing Commander should have been looking happier than he was about the whole thing, this would be good news for somebody, and yet he looked rather shamefaced and almost embarrassed. What a trauma it must have been for Jerome's parents to hear of their son's death. Yes, if it was Jerome, then it would be wonderful news, but could they stand a further shock! He thought of the terrible grief that Sarah Kate had suffered, and still suffered at the

83

loss of her husband, he had to find out for certain if Jerome was alive, and if he was then Sarah should be told immediately, as he knew that she would not have gone back to whatever secret work she was doing if she had been advised, she still must believe that her husband had died. She had to be informed if he was, indeed, alive, to stop her being overly reckless in the work she was doing, she *had* to know that Jerome would be here, waiting for her!

The drive to the hospital took forty five minutes, and Evan slept for forty three, it was as if his body knew that he would need that sleep in the hours to come.

Evan walked into the ward, and knew without doubt that it was Jerome who had survived the dreadful fireball and crash.

"Over here Evan, will you tell them who I am, so that I can come back with you?" Jerome called across the ward, and was 'shushed' by two nurses, and told to lie down, which he totally ignored. "Evan thank God you are here. How is Sarah Kate, did they tell her that I had been shot down in flames?"

"Yes, I'm afraid they did tell her, it looked as though you couldn't possibly have survived, your plane was a ball of fire going down."

"I guess the plane hit a tree and I was thrown out, and missed the inevitable explosion. I was knocked out cold, I guess for two or three days. It took me over a day to work my way out of the forest. I can vaguely remember the farmer in the truck I stopped nearly had a heart attack I was in such a dreadful state, and I remember very little. Where is Sarah, have you told her?" Jerome asked desperately, his eyes looked fine to Evan, not rolling or anything, just normal but desperate. He was bandaged quite a lot, but all he could think of was Sarah Kate.

"It seems like an awful long time ago, but she came to say goodbye to me yesterday afternoon. She said she was going away for a few weeks on a job." Evan said, wishing he could have done something more to stop her! Jerome looked totally let-down and frustrated by this information, and with a supreme effort, he then seemed to rally, he had to focus on becoming well again for his wife's return.

"Can you get Mrs Brown to keep my room Evan, I must be around when Sarah gets back, and she might call on Mrs Brown. The most important thing is to get her Wing Commander to get the information to her that I am alive. I don't believe she would have gone away again if this dreadful mix-up hadn't happened. We don't want her to take any unnecessary risks."

"She might well be away doing her Code and Cipher work, but they won't tell us anything because it is subject to the Official Secrets Act." Evan said in desperation, Jerome was not doing himself any favours, as he should rest and get well for Sarah Kate's return.

Jerome looked at his brother-in-law with disgust. "Yeh, you believe that just as much as I do Evan. I'm getting out of here as soon as I can, and then I'm going to find out whatever I can about what Sarah Kate is doing. She is my wife, and I know it must have been a terrible blow to be told I had been shot down. We are as close as you and Sarah Kate are, being twins, more so in a different way. I sense that she needs me." Jerome was now getting quite dangerously agitated, and Evan John tried to defuse the situation. He was in a ward full of other patients, and they could hear every word said.

"Leave it with me Jerome," Evan John whispered. "I'll do what I can, you concentrate of getting well. Sarah Kate slipped up slightly, after she heard you had been killed. I

85

insisted on walking her home, and I now know where she lives most of the time. I will see what I can find out."

"Well, what are you waiting for Evan?" Jerome said with a strong tinge of impatient exasperation!

"I have to ring our Wing Commander at the base, to confirm that *you,* Jerome Graham, are the John Doe pilot who turned up unexpectedly. Please give the Wing Commander time to get in touch with your parents, before *you* decide to ring them!" Evan John said equally exasperated, trying to see this situation from all angles!

"Oh yes, I should do that, they must have told all the family by now. Thanks Evan. I missed about five days before I came around and could tell them who I was. Do I look terrible Evan, will Sarah want to know me?" Jerome said looking at his bandaged arms and touching his head, with the three fingers that were not wrapped in bandages.

"If I am badly scarred, it might be better if I had died?" Jerome continued with an anxious look at Evan.

"Don't talk rot Jerome. Sarah will want you whatever you look like, and as far as I can see your face is fine, well no worse than usual, you have been lucky. In fact, I don't know anyone as lucky as you, although, my Uncle John did manage to come back from the dead too, in the last War."

"Evan, will you please go and make that telephone call, and then find out what you can about Sarah Kate? Come and collect me tomorrow, I must be around the RAF Base or Mrs Brown's just in case Sarah is able to contact me. You might as well use my car, if I still have one, until I can drive again," Jerome said. His eyebrows were almost joined together with the deep frown on his usually handsome face. Evan left the Ward shaking his head which was filled with complex thoughts and sensations. The poor nurses had with them a very impatient patient.

Evan doubted very much whether Jerome would be allowed to leave the hospital the next day. However, he did make the necessary telephone call, and then rejoined his car and driver for the return journey. Should he just walk up to the gate of the very large house into which Sarah Kate had disappeared? That was all he could do, he didn't know the name of the department in which she worked, or anything about what happened in that large house. First he would ask his Wing Commander if he could help in any way, and remembered how strangely he had behaved. They must see that Jerome's wife had a right to know that her husband was alive, wherever she was!

At the RAF base Evan John spent a good half hour celebrating the return of Jerome Graham from the dead! He had asked for an interview with their Wing Commander, and was relieved when this was granted immediately, and Evan could see that the officers were equally excited by this recent turn of good-fortune. However, when Evan requested some help with contacting Sarah Kate so that she might share the good news, the Wing Commander's expression turned uncompromising, and very official.

"I'm sorry, but I was informed yesterday when we were told that Flying Officer Graham might be alive, that we would not be able to contact his wife." The Wing Commander said, his eyes unfathomable, as he turned quickly away.

"Yesterday, you knew there was a possibility that the injured man *was* Flying Officer Jerome Graham. Sir, I saw my sister yesterday afternoon, she came to say 'goodbye' as she was leaving for a few weeks. There was no way that she could have left before early evening. Her Wing Commander *must* have let her leave without telling her there was a chance that her husband was alive, although he must have been aware of that fact!" Evan replied, not wanting to make an issue of the fact that the officer's reply was untruthful, but it was!

"That will be all, Flying Officer Evans." The Wing Commander said briskly, but Evan saw the truth of what he had said to the officer in his eyes, the look of unease, or guilt, was there once again! Evan saluted as a matter of course, and left slightly banging the door behind him, normally there would have been some sort of reprimand for such behaviour.

Evan John was furiously angry. He could not believe that they were being treated in this treacherous way. He and Jerome had been risking their lives every day when they flew in their Spitfires, along with the rest of their colleagues, and he believed that Sarah Kate was in all probability, taking similar risks! He needed to get Jerome out of hospital as soon as possible, they needed to stick together!

Three days later, Evan John and Jerome attempted to slip through the gates of the house where Evan had left a grieving Sarah Kate after escorting her home. They almost made it, but Jerome was a little slow and couldn't quite keep up with the delivery wagon they intended to follow, and Evan was also having a little trouble with his leg. Two Military Policemen escorted them around the back of the property, and they were left in a cell, in which was one chair only, and so Evan had to stand.

They were left to cool for four hours, where they plotted and planned but were unable to come up with any ideas as to how they might contact Sarah Kate! They were then handed printed notes to read, mainly specifying the Official Secrets Act 1911 Section Two under which it was a criminal offence to disclose information without lawful authority. The notes also explained that there were numerous reasons why many lives could be put in danger by their illegal and damaging actions - together with an Official Statement to sign, and each signature was to be witnessed by the other, and dated, then no further action would be taken against them, due to 'extenuating circumstances.' Nothing specific was said, but they were both intelligent young men and they signed, and were escorted out of the property, feeling inadequate and frustrated with their lot, and without seeing *anyone* except two Military Policemen. They did, however, feel quite relieved that Evan would be allowed to fly immediately, as would Jerome when he was declared fit enough.

One red cap looked at the other, and then towards the two men walking dispiritedly away from them, noting the flying boots and jackets on the two young men, also at Evan John's limp together with Jerome's bandaged body, and he shrugged with a resigned smile. "I hope they are better pilots than they are at breaking into Crown and Military property!"

The other one grinned, watching as the young men walked away quite slowly, to enable the bandaged one to keep up with the one with a limp. He was really envious of their ability and aptitude in learning new skills, as he would love to have been a pilot, but was too old, and probably was not brave enough anyway!

CHAPTER TEN

Mademoiselle Violette Marsaud waited at the bus stop in the small market town of Sainte Pierre in northern France trying to mingle with the locals, and only received a couple of interrogating glances from two of the older women, and Sarah assumed that this was only because she was not known to them. Everyone else seemed to be laughing and chatting, until silence reigned as a German armoured car passed by, and there were a couple of audible swear words, and then the talking started once again. She was glad of the thick coat which hid various items, but it matched in nicely with what the other women were wearing. Like them she had a scarf around her neck, and her basket of fresh autumn fruit was not out of place. The only item she was worried about was the knife tied securely to the outside of her thigh.

Marianne would be the one taking a risk, as she would be carrying the wireless set, Sarah's sleeve gun in a bunch of carrots, and the various components from which Sarah could construct the means by which to transmit Morse code, should she lose another wireless. Morse code was a system of communication in which letters of the alphabet and numbers could be represented by patterns of short and long signals, which could be conveyed as sound, flashes of light, written dots and dashes or the waving of flags, thankfully so far she had not had to use it. Sarah bought a ticket to Verneuil the nearest large town, and sat beside a window, and was soon squashed up, as a rather large woman sat down next to her, taking up most of the double seat. They did speak a few words to each other, and anyone watching would have assumed that they knew each other quite well, and Sarah Kate relaxed somewhat.

The bus arrived in Verneuil, and Sarah noticed that there was a market on in the main square. She had no idea where the Cafe Marsaud was situated, and regretted the oversight of not asking Marianne for precise directions from the bus stop. Marianne would be delivering fruit and vegetables there, together with the wireless set, but would not be in town for a while. She decided to get off the bus in the square, as most of the people that had come from Sainte Pierre had already done so. As a trained special operations executive, she was behaving abominably, how had she omitted to get precise directions from her colleagues?

Soon she was alone by the square, as everyone moved off quickly, as they at least knew their way around. She looked around cautiously. The only part she was familiar with in Verneuil was the area where they had managed to demolish the ammunitions store, a few months ago! She slowly turned wondering which way to go, and turned to find herself looking into the blue eyes of a German Officer. He bowed slightly and clicked his heels.

"Oberst Werner Muller," he introduced himself. "Can I help you mademoiselle, you appear to be lost?" he asked in perfect French.

"Cafe Marsaud if you please Herr Oberst?" She quaked in her shoes, but nobody would suspect, she presented a

91

serene expression to the Colonel. The man had very good manners, and seemed young to be a Colonel!

"That is my destination also, please follow me," he said, and Violette did, wondering if she was being watched, and by whom, and what would the watchers think? They walked along a street with a number of shops, into a square rather smaller than the market square, and he indicated 'Cafe Marsaud' across the square, and they walked on until they came to the cafe doorway, which he opened and indicated that she should precede him. She did, wondering what her 'cousin' Gerrard Marsaud would think. There was a bakery counter opposite the door, and just before them were six small tables with white tablecloths, each with a small vase with a flower in the middle, and two or three black painted chairs beside each table.

At one of the cafe tables sat a man reading a newspaper with the sleeves of his shirt rolled up, but he was facing Violette and she couldn't see if he had a sticking plaster on his elbow! Where was her 'cousin' Gerrard? She could hear voices in the room behind the shop and cafe, which must be the bakery.

"Gerrard, Gerrard are you there?" she called, it would be rather more than embarrassing if the man at the table came towards her – she should be able to recognise her own cousin, even whilst he was reading a newspaper!

A middle aged man came through the door to the cafe, wiping his hands on a cloth. He stopped short, with a gasp. "Violette, God Violette, it is you." He walked around the counter and pulled her into his arms in a big hug. He whispered in her ear 'somebody used up all the plasters.' He seemed to pull himself together with an effort, and looked towards Oberst Werner Muller.

"Herr Oberst, may I introduce my cousin from the countryside, Violette Marsaud. Tomorrow she will be

92

serving your coffee and croissants, and helping in the bakery."

Oberst Muller bowed slightly. "I was able to show your cousin the way here, she was lost."

"She has not visited for many years she must have been five or six when she last visited here, when my father was still alive." Gerrard said in explanation. "Sit down Violette, whilst I bring the coffee and croissants for Herr Oberst Muller."

Sarah sat at one of the tables, and waited for Gerrard to return to serve the German Colonel. Gerrard returned, and brought an elderly woman with him. She walked up to Violette, and as Violette stood up beside the table, she was hugged by the woman she assumed to be Gerrard's mother, and they moved off into the bakery, where the old women introduced herself as Aunt Bridgette. She looked around to see that they were alone. "Although you were expected, you frightened the life out of Gerrard, you look so much like his cousin Violette. It was a tragic loss to us all, but that will not be mentioned again. Now help yourself to coffee, and whatever else you want."

The shop door bell rang, and she hurried off into the shop. She served some customers and then returned to Violette. "I will show you your room, you have a visitor, I just saw her move through the garden to the back of the shop."

They went through the bakery into a comfortable living room, and a smaller kitchen. In between the two a flight of stairs led up to the other floors and 'aunt' Bridgette indicated she should go up two floors, and turn right. This she did, and came to her room. Marianne was sitting on the small single bed.

"I saw you walking through the town with Oberst Muller, he is in charge of the men at the Chateau Genevieve. He

93

comes here most mornings for coffee and croissants. Is everything alright?" Marianne asked her brows furrowed with worry.

"Everything is fine, he saw me looking lost, and showed me the way to the Cafe Marsaud. I stupidly forgot to ask you for directions to the Café from the bus stop. He saw me being greeted by my 'cousin' Gerrard, so I guess he will accept that is who I am."

"Oberst Werner Muller is a gentleman. Not like some of the other German Officers who have just arrived at the Chateau, Jean says the new arrivals are Gestapo, and we will have to be ultra careful in future. Since they arrived in Verneuil the whole atmosphere has changed. Gerrard says you can have the wireless upstairs in the loft, there is no light, and he has left candles and matches. Either myself or Jean will come into the cafe in a few days if there is anything to be coded and passed on to London. Otherwise you just settle in, and you will soon be accepted without question." She patted Sarah on the shoulder, and quickly left.

Next morning, looking smart in a black dress and white apron, Sarah *did* serve coffee and croissants to Oberst Werner Muller. In the next few days, she noted that there were very few days that he missed calling at the Cafe Marsaud.

Sarah did settle in, and a lot of the information that she coded and sent to London in the next six weeks did not make much sense to her, but she hoped that it did to the boffins in London. No doubt, together with information from other Resistance Groups things became clear!

She became quite good a slipping notes into partly sliced buns, for Jean or Marianne, and equally adept at receiving notes and deciphering them when the goods were paid for. She never used the wireless from the roof space at the cafe more than a few minutes a fortnight, and changed the days and time on every occasion. She moved, on her days off from the Cafe, to a small boathouse on a river, where the second wireless was hidden and she used that. On those occasions an old man sat on the side of the river beside a bridge, sometimes fishing, sometimes not. He never acknowledged her, but for some reason she assumed that he was keeping watch over her, and she relaxed just a little, knowing he was near, but she did not stay very long.

A number of times after a weekend, when the Chateau was full to the brim with resting officers, now mostly Gestapo, there was a lot of information. Occasionally Sarah coded this, and it was taken away by Jean to be sent to London via another Resistance Group. She often wondered who was collecting this information which was handed to the Resistance. Just before these weekends Gerrard delivered to the Chateau Genevieve large orders from the Bakery, which was very good for business, but he always came back worried and depressed. One or two young women had been going up to the Chateau for dinner, a drink, and some dancing, at the request of the German Officers, this had worked quite well as Oberst Muller had arranged for the young women to be driven home each time, and the promise that the Colonel had made to the Mayor of Verneuil had been upheld. Now it seemed that some of the girls were not too eager to be brought home, and the Gestapo Officers were even less inclined for this to happen.

Things seemed to calm down slightly when a number of 'ladies' of questionable virtue arrived in the town, this quietened down some of the parents of the youngsters of Verneuil. However, this did not last very long. The imported 'ladies' of questionable virtue seemed to tar the girls of Verneuil with the same brush. The very sad thing was that some of the young women who went to the Chateau went under duress, as they were worried about any repercussions that might be suffered by their families, and some of these girls were also reviled by the local townspeople!

One Friday Gerrard met one of his oldest friends, it was questionable whether or not he had been away to join-up, and then after the Armistice he had returned home, or where he had been? However, his return was celebrated, rather too much and the outcome of this was that Gerrard, slightly inebriated, managed to fall down the cellar steps and dislocate his shoulder. Luckily all the baking had been done, but he was unable to drive the baking order up to the Chateau. Violette was the only one who could drive the old car, and it fell to her to do the delivery. She was unlucky that when delivering the trays of buns and cakes, she was seen by one of the Gestapo Officers, and he held her by the arm arrogantly, and she had to stop.

"You are very pretty, and we are short of female company this evening. You will come into the Chateau with me. I am Oberleutnant Heinrich Schiller it is your lucky day. We will find you something nice to wear, suitable to have dinner with me." His attitude was making her angry as he stood tall and arrogantly before her, and when his hold on her arm lightened she made her move.

She managed to reach the car before he realised that she intended to ignore his instructions and return to town, but a car came up the drive, and she missed her chance. She was manhandled by Oberleutnant Heinrich Schiller, none too gently, back into the Chateau, and the car keys were taken from her. Schiller was watching her with his cold blue eyes surrounded by blonde lashes as she slowly climbed up the stairs, when she was shocked to be met by a young woman, Marianne Flamand! Neither acknowledged the other and Schiller insisted that Marianne should take Violette upstairs and make sure she was given something nice to wear instead of her black and white waitress outfit.

A dark haired woman came along the landing towards them. "I am Isabelle, and this is Marianne, I understand you have to get changed. Come into this room, and get changed, choose something off that rail. What is your name?"

"Violette Marsaud, from the Bakery, I was just delivering provisions."

"Well, you should have kept out of sight. Now you will have to stay, now that Heinrich Schiller has said so, he is very unpredictable, and doesn't give a damn about Oberst Muller's promise to the Mayor of Verneuil. Try to keep a low profile, and you might manage to get away without incident." Isabelle said, and Violette surmised that Isabelle must work at the Chateau, as she was very familiar with the place and seemed very confident, although she appeared to be carrying out the wishes of the Gestapo.

Sarah moved towards the rail and found a dress which seemed to cover more flesh that most of the others. She glanced at Marianne but she was looking the other way, and discussing something with Isabelle. Sarah was shocked to see Marianne here, she had imagined that she kept a low profile like herself, and she also wondered if Jacques and Jean were aware of what Marianne was doing! The large amount of information that Sarah had coded and sent to London must come from somewhere!

The dining room was very big, and the biggest table held about thirty covers, and most of the Gestapo Officers were already sitting there. There was a smaller round table, and that seemed to be occupied by the German soldiers. Oberleutnant Schiller was purposefully moving towards Sarah to claim her as his companion, when Sarah was shocked and relieved when her elbow was taken, and she was pulled towards the round table.

"Mademoiselle Violette will be dining with me," Oberst Werner Muller said clearly with conscious authority, and after a second of indecision, Oberleutnant Schiller shrugged his shoulders angrily, and reluctantly moved back to the Gestapo filled table. Schiller was furious, *he* had forced that girl into the Chateau, she was a really pretty and the fact that she appeared cool and collected was an added bonus, he was looking forward with pleasure to taking that haughty smile off her face, and he would make sure that she enjoyed herself, and then she would come back for more! Now the Oberst (Colonel) was pulling rank. An ordinary Oberst was no better than a Gestapo Oberleutnant (First Officer) in his opinion, and he would, in time, get his own back on Oberst Muller and that haughty woman!

"What are you doing here Violette?" Werner Muller asked in a shocked voice.

"I just came to deliver trays of buns and cakes, as Gerrard has dislocated his shoulder, and I got dragged in here against my will by Oberleutnant Schiller." She said angrily, and looked into his blue eyes which were kind, but also warned her to be careful what she said. She had become used to him calling her by the name Violette, this he did most mornings in the Cafe Marsaud. She was a little surprised that he didn't say anything to Schiller, he was the Colonel wasn't he, the highest rank in the Chateau!

"Enjoy your meal Violette, and ignore the other table. It is not a good idea to anger the Gestapo, it looks as though all the soldiers, including myself, will be moved from the Chateau in the next week or two, probably to the Russian Front, and more Gestapo will be living here, and it is possible German SS Troops too. They did a sweep of the area a few weeks back, and will return. Verneuil will not be the same." He spoke quietly, so that only Violette could hear him, and she realised this was a warning that she should not forget, and which Werner Muller probably meant for Gerrard Marsaud and the whole town. He was just a soldier following orders, and it seemed that many of those orders were not to his liking, or the liking of many of the ordinary German soldiers fighting for their country!

Sarah wasn't sure how he managed it, but somehow after dinner, and before the music began the car keys arrived on her side plate. She pocketed them, and looked her thanks towards Werner Muller. He started to move to a standing position, and whispered. "Go whilst I draw attention elsewhere."

He moved over to the small area where three musicians were tuning up their instruments ready to start playing, and everyone looked his way. Sarah quietly slipped away from the table, and turned briefly closing the door behind her carefully. She had caught the glance of Isabelle who was sitting at the top of the large table. Isabelle turned away to look at Oberst Werner Muller as he spoke briefly introducing the musicians. Sarah sighed with relief and ran to her car. She would have to be provided with a new black dress and white apron, as far as she was concerned the clothes she had arrived at the Chateau in, had gone forever. She parked the car behind the Bakery, and went in to give Gerrard and his mother the information about the ordinary German troops being sent elsewhere, and more Gestapo and German SS troops would be arriving. Gerrard was angry that she had been accosted and forced into the Chateau, but realised he couldn't do anything about it, but promised to accompany her if she had to make any further deliveries.

Sarah fervently hoped that the local doctor would manage to relocate Gerrard's shoulder without too much discomfort, as she was well aware that she should keep a very low profile, and definitely keep away from Oberleutnant Heinrich Schiller, who would like nothing better than to humiliate her.

It did occur to her that not only had she made a dangerous enemy, but so had Oberst Werner Muller, and she hoped he would be able to leave the area quickly.

Next morning very early, she made her way to the boathouse, to send a message to London. The elderly French gentleman was sitting beside the bridge and she wondered if he slept there – it was only six thirty in the dewy morning. Why was he there so early? Was he keeping an eye on Violette for the Resistance, or someone else, and should she start to worry? Perhaps she should ask Jean Distelle, he seemed to be in charge of this immediate area of the Resistance. On the other hand she was supposed to keep a very low profile, and not stir matters up in the immediate area. Also for what reason had Marianne been in the Chateau?

CHAPTER ELEVEN

For the next few mornings, the bakery order for the Chateau, was again delivered by Violette Marsaud, but she was accompanied by her cousin, who was still nursing a very sore shoulder. No further deliveries were made in the evening, except when Gerrard was available.

Violette continued to receive information from Jean Distelle as she worked in the Cafe and Bakery, and she worried and wondered whether Marianne was still visiting the Chateau. Her main concern was whether Jean Distelle and Jacques Flamand were aware of her activities, as she believed that if they did they would certainly not approve. On the other hand, was Marianne one of the most prolific providers of information from the Chateau, if so she must be one of the most valued members of the Resistance? Jean was probably still blaming himself for the fact that the German SS had killed his father, and Jacques must feel lousy because he had been unable to save Monsieur Distelle, and had been beaten very badly himself! London did not give much away and kept their communications with Sarah minimal for obvious reasons, but she was asked to pass on to the Resistance Group their approval and thanks.

During the long evenings living at the Cafe Marsaud, Sarah Kate did have a tendency to restlessness, and she would walk back and forth worrying about Evan John although she *felt* that he was alright, and grieving for the loss of Jerome. She wished that she had been able to bring with her just one little photograph so that she could make sure that she never forgot his expressive and loving face. She wondered how long it would be before she again visited Rowan Trees, and her family, and one of her biggest regrets was the fact that she had never been able to introduce her husband to her family - Megs would have been so envious of her handsome husband. She missed the valley where everyone knew and helped everyone – all the occupants were like one close knit family.

Oberst Werner Muller still came to the Cafe for his coffee and croissants most mornings, and always had a few words for Violette. During these brief conversations she learned that he had a beautiful Swiss wife and two daughters, none of whom he had seen since nineteen thirty eight, and he missed them terribly. Sarah was not surprised, but glad to realise that not all Germans were Nazis, nor did all of them approve of the Gestapo and SS troops. At least Evan John and all his colleagues and the men from the valley who were fighting for their country and for freedom, all believed that they were fighting for a just cause!

One morning Sarah was serving Jean, and providing him with his change and a small message from London, when she felt the hairs on the back of her head stand up, something was very wrong. It was - not with the transaction between her and Jean, but because Heinrich Schiller was standing immediately behind Jean.

Heinrich Schiller stared at her. His eyes were as blue as Werner Muller's but cold and calculating, and she realised that he was as shocked as she was. He had never associated the delivery girl he had forced into the Chateau with the Cafe Marsaud. She wondered what this would mean for her cousin and his family. He ordered coffee, and sat at a table in the middle of the room, where she continually had to walk around him. It was a war of nerves, and she thought *he* must be winning. His narrowed eyes seemed to move around the room after her, and she felt like a mouse caught in a trap, and she wanted to scream. Eventually he finished his coffee and left, and she sighed with relief.

The relief she felt was not felt for very long, as when she was sending a wireless message to London the next night from the attic, she heard the screech of car tyres outside the bakery which had been closed for a couple of hours. She managed to dismantle the wireless and hide it in a wall cavity made for that purpose, but she didn't have the time to climb down from the attic, and she laid down between the floor joists carefully and silently as possible to hide, covering herself with a number of flour sacks, and cardboard boxes. She could hear the disturbance downstairs, and quite soon she heard heavy footsteps coming up the stairs, and the voice of Madame Masaud berating the Germans, trying desperately to get them to return downstairs.

Soon the trapdoor was pushed open, and a light was shone around the roof space, all the time Madame Marsaud was berating Oberleutnant Heinrich Schiller, Leutnant Wilhelm Schmidt, and his two companions who were searching the property. Gerrard was visiting friends and was not at home, she informed the searching Germans, and his cousin Violette was with him, but she was ignored.

"If you are not careful you will fall through the ceiling between the joists, be careful, you are damaging our property. My son will complain to Oberst Muller if you are not more careful." Her voice was shrill, and Sarah knew that the old woman was sure that Sarah would be discovered, and they would all be shot. "I told you so," she screamed as one of Schiller's feet came through the ceiling just to the side of the trap door above her head, and she was covered in lime and debris as was the landing floor.

"Be quiet women," Schiller shouted in German, and he extracted his foot from the ceiling. He flashed a knife in the light from his torch, "I will just make sure there's nobody hiding amongst all these used sacks and papers."

Sarah was in total darkness under the sacks, and only partly protected by the wooden joists. The flour and sugar sacks were dusty, and she was concentrating upon keeping herself from sneezing or coughing. She heard the rip of cloth as the knife was slashed at the sacks, then once again, and then she bit her lip to stop herself from screaming as the knife sliced into her thigh. She thought she must have stopped breathing with the pain, and then Schiller was moving back to the trapdoor, and slowly lowering himself down onto the dust and lime strewn landing floor. As Schiller didn't say anything, she assumed that any blood from her wound had not started to flow until after the knife was retracted, or it had been left on the sacks. She gripped her thigh tightly and felt a wet and warm stickiness, and she felt very sick.

Schiller was furiously angry that his search had been in vain, he really wanted to bring trouble and strife to this family. He was truly attracted to the young cousin, and was determined that if he couldn't have her then Oberst Werner Muller wouldn't either. This family needed to be taught a lesson, as did the Oberst.

"We will look in the cellars now," he said with determination, whilst the old women stood with wide eyes filled with shock. "Mind out of my way woman," Schiller pushed her aside and followed his colleagues down towards the cellar steps.

Madame Marsaud stared at the red stain slowly increasing in size on the ceiling above her. There was nothing she could do until the Gestapo officers had left the building, she would have to get help for she couldn't pull herself through the trap door, as having steps on the landing would have been a dead give away. She followed the Germans downstairs, with a prayer on her quivering lips for the girl she was becoming very fond of since the death of the real Violette.

As soon as Schiller had disappeared through the trap door, and she could hear footsteps going downstairs, Sarah let out a long breath, and sat up carefully in the very dim light from the small skylight on the roof, dislodging the dusty sacks.

She managed to pull her dress over her head, followed by her underskirt, and then she pulled on her dress. She tore the underskirt into two strips, then the rest she folded into a pad, and then tied the strips tightly around her left thigh. Thank goodness it was the left thigh, she could in the future still have her knife strapped to her right thigh – she was right handed. Her fingers were sore with trying to rip the cotton underskirt, as she had taken the knife from her thigh when she had started to speak to London, because her next plan had been to go to bed!

She had been enjoying a sort of comfort zone, and she had become complacent, but now Schiller had changed all that. He seemed determined to cause trouble for her and her family, she realised now that she thought of them as her *family*, if only temporarily! She was sure that Schiller's visit to the bakery had been out of spite not because he really thought there was anything to find. Surely Madame Marsaud and Gerrard would not have anything to hide in the cellar! Now her thigh was attended to in a fashion, she crawled to the open trap door, and listened. She heard a very angry Oberleutnant Heinrich Schiller vacate the cafe with a very loud and angry bang of the shop door, followed by a furious tirade of vitriolic abuse from Madame Bridgette Marsaud.

Sarah Kate gave a sigh of relief as the vehicle left the vicinity of the Cafe. She was just lowering herself through the trap door, when Gerrard's mother came puffing up the stairs. Sarah was hanging suspended with her whole weight on her arms, as usually she jumped down but didn't know if she could manage to jump onto one leg without doing further damage. Madame Marsaud helped Sarah down and then into her bedroom, and then rushed off to get all the bandages she could find, and means to clean the long knife wound. When the temporary bandages had been removed, the cut appeared to be quite deep and at least six inches long.

She had to go to the local doctor to get the wound stitched, and said that she had fallen in the bakery, knocking over a table on which was a very sharp knife, and he stared at her for a moment, he didn't ask any more questions, only told her that the stitches should be taken out in about five to seven days.

The next morning Oberst Werner Muller arrived at the cafe, and was disappointed to find that Violette was not serving in the cafe and shop.

He had almost finished his coffee when Madame Marsaud informed him that the whole household had been upset because of the damaging search that Oberleutnant Heinrich Schiller and three colleagues had made the night before of the cafe and house. She told him that Schiller had put his foot through the ceiling, and had damaged a lot of stores which were kept in the cellar. She complained that there was nothing to find, and no reason why this should have happened!

Oberst Muller was quite upset, and all he could do was apologise. He tried to explain that the Gestapo were a law unto them selves, and there was little that he could do, as he and his men would be moving away within a week or so.

The next day he was relieved to find Violette serving his coffee and croissants, and everything back to normal in the Cafe and Bakery. However, Oberst Muller was very much aware of the overbearing attitude, and antipathy felt by the Gestapo to the ordinary German soldiers billeted at the Chateau. He and his men hoped that they would be moved shortly, but that would leave the people of Verneuil with a highly volatile and unsympathetic invasive Gestapo and SS force.

Sarah had to take it easy for a while. The local doctor had cleaned and dressed her wound, and she felt that too many people might assume her involvement with the Resistance if they found out about her injury. In addition to the doctor there was the plasterer and his mate, who had come to the Cafe to plaster the ceiling where Schiller had put through his foot, and where it had to be taken down because it was stained with her blood! Also there was the old French gentleman who seemed to be around whenever she had to use the wireless secreted in the boathouse. She was vitally aware that she might be putting these local and helpful citizens in danger.

She was now totally accepted as Violette Marsaud, and she realised that only the very close family were aware of what the real Violette Marsaud had suffered at the hands of the Germans, and the reason she had taken her own life.

She had spoken with Oberst Werner Muller only this morning in the cafe, and he had seemed downcast as he was expecting to be sent to the Russian Front together with his men. She noted this as news which might interest London. However, Sarah felt very confused. She now looked upon the Oberst as a friend, as he was both encouraging and sympathetic with regard to the combustible and vitriolic situation between Violette and Oberleutnant Heinrich Schiller. Werner Muller, who often spoke lovingly of his wife and daughter's was also the enemy, but she remembered that he had given a clear and kindly warning that the Gestapo would be taking over completely in the town and to tread carefully - how could this be?

Since the search of the Cafe and Bakery, and her injury caused by Heinrich Schiller without his knowledge, Sarah had taken to wearing her knife on her thigh at all times, and if it were undetectable she would also take her sleeve gun with her. She knew that if she was searched and either item was found she would be in deep trouble, but since being stabbed by Schiller, she was determined to be ready for any further such confrontation. Her secret worry was that although she had been trained to defend herself, even in silent killing, if that situation arose would she be able to maim or take the life of another human being?

She was very worried because at times she awakened during the night, after a bad dream, and she thought she disturbed herself with her own voice. These dreams were often about Evan John, or Jerome, and she realised that she must not sleep anywhere that her sleeping habits could endanger any of her friends, colleagues, or adopted family Marsaud. She only had to speak in English during her sleep and she would be in deep trouble, and so would they!

Months and months had rushed by, and now she was glad of her thick coat, which kept her warm and camouflaged her silhouette, which during the summer she had worried about the odd bulge being discernible (and this was not due to her body), she had lost weight over the months.

Oberst Werner Muller had been given his 'marching orders,' he and his men were to leave within the month. Sarah was not sure what she felt about this, she would miss Werner Muller - he was the only gentlemanly German she had met. In all honesty he was the only German that she had got to know at all. She was confused, and hoped that he would manage to return to his Swiss wife and his two daughters in due course. She also wondered if, by informing London of this event, she might be putting him in danger!

She felt depressed, she was worried about Werner who had helped her when Schiller had forced her to stay at the Chateau, and she longed to hear at some time soon that the men of the valley fighting with the Border Regiment, and her brother Evan John were all safe and well. It was a very confusing part of her life, but apparently, all was fair in love and war and except for the love of her family and country, *war* was the only thing left for Sarah Kate!

CHAPTER TWELVE

In December 1941 the whole town of Verneuil was shocked when news reached them that the Japanese had bombed Pearl Harbour, Hawaii. Now the United States of America were therefore drawn into the War, and declared War on Japan. It seemed that the whole War was escalating without control, and the French seemed to think that the Americans would now declare War on Germany. Since early 1941 the Americans had moved troops into Greenland, because of the Atlantic convoys and German reconnaissance flights in the North Atlantic. If they did now get more involved in Europe then they would surely be welcome.

Months later Violette left the Cafe Marsaud on one of her usual evening walks. She passed the elderly gentlemen near the bridge, and made her way to the boathouse. Communicating with London only took a few minutes, as London had warned her she must keep any communications as short as possible, and she had supplied them with a lot of information in the last two weeks, and now was glad to be heading home to bed.

She leaned over to pick up a tree branch from next to the path thinking if it was painted white it would make a nice Christmas decoration with a few ribbon bows, for the Café's next Christmas. Her heart nearly stopped as she paused. The elderly French gentleman lay before her, his eyes stared up at the darkening sky and were blank and protruding, and there were marks of a garrotte around his throat. It must only have been a couple of seconds before she managed to stand upright again and continue on her way. He had become very familiar to her although they had never acknowledged each other or spoken. She wiped away a tear and her heart ached for him. He had looked grotesque and she felt for his family, and it must be all *her* fault! She was certain he had been protecting her and the spare wireless. However, Jean or Jacques and Marianne had never mentioned him. Her heart was racing loudly in her anxiety, and she felt quite dizzy, and took in a deep breath of evening air.

She managed to walk at her usual speed along the river path, although she wanted to run, and a loud scream would have helped. As she neared the bridge she noticed a German armoured car parked at the end of the bridge, and the lights were suddenly switched on, and she gasped as her heart thudded in shock. She was horrified to see her worst nightmare - Oberleutnant Schiller climbed out of the driving seat. He stood before her with arms akimbo with his legs slightly apart, and there was just enough light for her to see the expression in the blue eyes of indomitable power, and the sneer on his thin lips was hateful. She had no doubt that he was the perpetrator of the murder of her old protector. He was vile, and she felt a deep antipathy running through her veins.

Again in only a couple of seconds she realised that he would not let her get away from him and he would probably grab her by the arms. She stumbled a little, as if in fear and trepidation of his intentions, which she *did* feel, and knelt before him for a second. In that second she managed to dislodge from her right coat arm, the sleeve gun into the grass at the side of the road. He then grabbed her by the left arm and smiled in arrogant triumph, hauling her towards the armoured car, and into the passenger seat. He was arrogantly confident and didn't notice what she had done, and she breathed again, but her relief was to be short-lived.

"Aha, my little sweetheart, we meet again, and we shall have dinner together, then dance, and that will only be the start of a very satisfying night," he spoke in German and was not aware that she understood him. However, she *was* frightened, and looked so, and that seemed to please him, and he drove off at speed.

One of the things that she had been taught during her months of hard training, in the North of Scotland, was that killing could make a person feel more sexually dominant, and she literally quaked at the idea, particularly with regard to the arrogant and vile man in the driving seat. Her thoughts quickly returned to the *real* Violette Marsaud, and she began to realise the sheer terror and pain the young girl must have suffered at the hands of her attackers.

Gravel scattered as he swung the armoured car around the drive to the Chateau, screeching to a sudden stop. He grabbed her arm and hauled her from the passenger seat straight across the driving seat, and when she was standing beside him he slammed the door shut, and her arm started to become numb due to his hand stopping her blood flow. "You are not getting away from me this time, and Madame Isabelle will make sure you look especially pretty for me." His grin was triumphant, and inwardly she seethed with rage.

Schiller hurried Sarah through the imposing doors of the Chateau, and hurried her up to the first floor, where he hammered on a door. About twenty seconds later, the door was opened by an angry looking Isabelle.

"Madame Isabelle, you will kindly get Violette ready to have dinner, she needs to show off her nice curves, so that my friends will be suitably jealous. Herr Oberst Muller was careless and she managed to get away, but *I* will not be so careless." He sounded really malicious and Sarah wondered what Isabelle's position was in the Chateau, and was glad that Schiller thought that she had managed to escape without any help on her last 'visit' to the Chateau, she was also well aware that Isabelle had watched her leave, when Oberst Muller had demanded attention in the dining room. Schiller clicked his heels in mock respect, and hurried towards the stairs, with a satisfied and almost proud expression on his arrogant face which Sarah was determined to wipe off at the earliest opportunity.

"Madame why do you do this?" Sarah asked as she could see from the woman's face that she was angry and tense.

"Get a dress off that rail, and start making yourself ready," Isabelle said brusquely. "I don't have any choice, my husband is bedridden upstairs. The Chateau is our home, requisitioned by the Germans, and I cannot leave my husband. Do not make things difficult for me Violette. Your only hope tonight is to pray that Oberleutnant Schiller gets too much to drink, and becomes incapable, you must *encourage* him to drink. Make eyes at him, or tease him, whatever it takes. Hopefully by morning he will not know how and when you got away."

Sarah stared at Isabelle with dismay, and wondered if Marianne would be here this evening, or just the 'ladies' of questionable virtue! Surely Marianne was not one of those, however much she wanted the downfall of the Gestapo for the killing of Monsieur Distelle and the beating of her brother Jacques?

Sarah dressed in a red wine coloured dress, and Isabelle took the pins from her hair, and Sarah was relieved to have it taken out of the severe plait.

"You look really beautiful with your hair down Violette, perhaps we should plait it again! On the other hand you should be able to make sure that he gets more than enough to drink, he will be too busy looking at you."

"Oberst Werner Muller, will he be around, he let me slip away unnoticed last time?" Sarah asked, she had seen him in the Cafe yesterday, but not today.

"He is a gentleman, but since getting news that they are to leave, he now spends most of his time alone, or with one or two of his Officers who dine with him upstairs. It is just as well, as the Gestapo Officers anger him, and I am afraid that he angers them also, and he is better out of their sight."

Sarah was bitterly disappointed, last time she had been forced here Oberst Muller had saved her, but tonight he didn't even know she was here – neither did Gerrard or the Resistance. Would they have found the old Frenchman's body, near the riverside, had anyone seen her leaving, and would they be looking for Violette? She was virtually on her own, but that was what she had been trained for wasn't it?

Isabelle walked down the grand staircase with Sarah, and they paused at the bottom of the stairs. "You could make a run for it Violette, and I *would* give the alarm. I could not do anything else, or my husband and I would suffer, and probably our home and tenants. Also, you should think of your family in Verneuil."

"I do think of my family Isabelle, and thank you for your advice."

Yes she did think of her families, both at home in England, and at the Cafe in Verneuil. But she longed for her husband, and wondered if he would be waiting for her to join him by the end of this night – possibly in a few hours

114

everything would be resolved, she really didn't think any suffering would be worse than she had suffered on hearing of his death – and so she didn't have anything to worry about!

Oberleutnant Schiller made a big thing of Violette coming to join him at the table, and from then on it continued going downhill. Sarah lost count of the drinks he took from the small glass of Schnapps in front of him which was filled up as soon as he downed it in one go. She slowly sipped only wine, and made sure that her glass was not filled up very often. She ate whatever was put in front of her because she was not used to drinking alcohol but could not avoid it this evening. As far as she could see the drinking did not seem to affect Schiller very much. However, as the evening went on he became more familiar, and he started to put his hand on her knee, or his hateful arm around her shoulders. She started to worry, her only weapon was the knife and that was tied to her right thigh, and she was blessed as she was sitting on his right side, and he nudged her left thigh with his right knee. It was imperative - she *had* to get him drunk and incapable.

Schiller introduced her to the Second Officer who was sitting on her right, whose voice she remembered from their visit to the Cafe Marsaud when Schiller had stabbed her in the thigh. He was introduced as Leutnant Wilhelm Schmidt, and he was a grade below Schiller and this was made plain by the way the Leutnant tried to please Schiller at every turn. Leutnant Schmidt put his hand on her knee at one stage when Schiller was occupied by the woman on his other side. His hand was removed and her elbow made him wince – if he was looking for a threesome he was out of luck. The next time he tried anything she would remember what she had been taught, and he would be in much greater pain. She turned back to find Schiller's hard blue eyes on her, and he looked pleased and excited, and anticipation of a rough, pleasurable, long and satisfying night shone in his cold blue eyes.

If she ran for the doorway in front of all these people, would she be allowed to leave, what was the worst they could do, shoot her as a spy? She looked around the table and wondered. Everyone, including Schiller and Isabelle all believed she was Violette Marsaud surely someone would come to her aid, a young woman from a well known local family! She sighed, whatever she did would recoil on her family - any punishment would be suffered by the family Marsaud. She gave Schiller a cool dismissive smile, thinking she would try and disable him if he tried to attack her, surely even the Germans would think he had received his just deserts. Her smile warmed slightly, and she placed his full glass before him, as she did many more times during the next two hours.

A little later, Isabelle watched Violette carefully. It did not seem that the young girl was drunk, she had done well. Violette was held by Oberleutnant Schiller, and Schiller was supported by Leutnant Wilhelm Schmidt as they staggered up the stairs. Wilhelm Schmidt seemed only slightly intoxicated, and Isabelle made a point of talking to him, in order that Schiller and Violette could make their escape. Isabelle really thought that what she was doing was correct, and Violette had at least a *chance* against *one* intoxicated man! Isabelle did not notice one of the doors open across the passageway, and a slight gasp, and then it close again.

In Verneuil an elderly Frenchman's body had been found. It had been found by a young couple on their way home along the riverside. The terrified screams could still be heard of the young woman, as her family tried to comfort her. Groups of locals in their sleeping attire were discussing this event. Meanwhile a young boy had been sent to the Cafe

Marsaud, by a very angry Jean Distelle, but the boy's first call was to be to the son of the murdered man.

Jean himself slipped quietly away, and made his way to the boathouse, he must remove the wireless equipment. He was feeling anguish for the death of another of the elderly population caused by this dreadful War, and a deep foreboding. Would he see Violette Marsaud again, or should the whole Resistance Group be disbanded for the foreseeable future?

Schiller turned the lock in the door, and turned Violette around, trapping her arms against her sides, he kissed her until he became sexually aroused. She tried not to shudder too much from the distaste she felt. He removed his arms and she wanted to wipe her mouth, but dare not. She looked into his arrogant eyes and doubted if he had consumed enough to make him go to sleep. Maybe he had drunk sufficient to make his reflexes slow down, she had to hope so. His eyes darkened, as he looked up and down her body. He took off his uniform jacket and started on his belt.

"I'm going to enjoy undressing you Violette, and I will make you enjoy it too, I never get complaints you should note." He paused, "I'm thirsty, get me a drink."

"Of course," she said almost pleasantly, anything to stall him. She walked to a dressing table and lifted a bottle of Schnapps.

"No not that, water."

"Alright, I think there is some over there," she said pointing to a jug with a piece of lace covering it with small beads holding it down. She had to pass the door to get to the jug, and she turned the key in the lock as silently as she could - she might need to get out of this room quickly, and she glanced at the tall window with heavy brocade curtains decorated with tassels, and realised they were on at least the second floor, maybe the third! She lifted the jug, it was full of water. She pretended she couldn't hold the weight of it with one hand, having the glass in the other, and the jug slipped spreading water around the floor.

"Damn, I've spilled the water, I'll just wipe it up off the floor," she said in the local language which had become natural to her, and he stretched out on the bed with a grumble. He was now naked and she gasped in horror. She had seen Evan John naked as a boy, but the only *man* she had seen naked was her husband Jerome, and he was the only man she would ever want!

She hated to part with her small but lethal knife, but she could not keep it strapped to her thigh! She slipped it into her hand, and slowly started to unbutton her dress with the other hand. The dress dropped to the floor and she picked it up and walked towards the bed. She started to fold up the dress tidily and she saw from the anticipation in his blue eyes, that he thought she was teasing him, and she slipped the knife underneath the dress, and slowly placed the knife and dress at the bottom of the large bed. She gazed at the man on the bed and strived not to show how much she reviled his arrogant and bestial face.

"Get over here girl, and stop teasing," Schiller said, and she could tell that the drink had not affected him very much. She looked at the lamp beside the bed, and wondered if that might be heavy enough to knock him out.

Suddenly she was grabbed with a hand on each of her upper arms, and she was pulled onto the bed and he had turned her on to her back, and she was caged by his heavy body. She managed to get one hand free and scratched his face, and felt and heard a loud slap as he hit her, and she thought she screamed. Her head seemed to ring with the force of the blow - whatever happened she must not pass out.

He trapped one arm with his knee, and sneered as he looked down into her bruised face, he held her other arm with his, and ripped at her remaining clothing with his right arm. She put every last bit of strength into a sudden movement, she put her feet flat on the bed with knees bent and thrust up her hips and unbalanced him. She had one arm free and stabbed her fingers into his eyes, and he howled with pain. She was amazed that he didn't let her go, and she reeled from another slap against her temple, and her head felt as if it would split with the pain. She shouted angrily trying to build up her strength, ready for another concerted attack – he was more than twice her size, and young and very fit. She stared into his now bloodshot tyrannical eyes, thinking they were the last things she might see in this world.

Suddenly she was free, Schiller was being pulled back from her body by a uniformed arm across his throat, and one arm was bent up his back. He was hurled across the room and landed with a thump against the door. He crawled back to his feet angrily.

Oberst Werner Muller just for a second glanced at Violette to see if she was alright, and her wide open horrified eyes and hoarse gasp, warned him that Schiller was attacking him from behind.

Schiller had landed on the floor, near to his clothing, and now he held his knife above his head and brought it down towards Werner Muller and stabbed him in the side of his chest. Werner turned and saw the hate in Schiller's eyes, as Schiller pulled the knife out of his chest, and it was being lowered again with intent to kill – Werner rolled but knew he had little chance of getting away as his body was wracked with pain, and he waited for the second blow of the knife. This all seemed to be happening in slow motion. The blow didn't reach him, and when he turned holding the wound in his side, he saw why. Violette had stabbed Schiller with a

119

small knife, but it was placed in his back where it was certain to kill. Werner Muller stared at her horrified face, he thought she was going to scream but he watched with amazement as she slowly got command of her emotions. With indomitable strength of purpose she looked at Werner with tears in her eyes, her shocking words were simple and to the point.

"He was going to kill you, just for pulling him off me! Look what *he made* me do." She looked down at Schiller's limp body. "He shouldn't have done any of this, it's barbaric." She moved to the bed and pulled a sheet, tearing off a strip, wondering where the strength to do this had come from!

She folded it into a pad, and helped Werner to his feet, as he looked at her closely. He was waiting for her to dissolve into tears or start to scream. His uniform jacket was already open, and she pulled at his shirt until she could place the pad against his body to stem the bleeding, and then with another strip of sheet she wrapped it around his chest and tied it securely. She had looked at the wound, not knowing how deep it was, but it didn't seem too bad, there was more blood coming from Schiller's body where she had stabbed him in the back. Later she would think of Schiller as someone's son, husband or daddy, but for now he was just dead meat, better him than Werner, as Werner was a good and caring man.

She pushed Werner's shirt back into place, and slipped her arms around his body. "Thank you for saving me, he was too strong, even the drink didn't seem to have any effect on him." There was a slight tremor in her voice, but it was only because she nearly choked because of how much she had hated being close to Schiller! Almost as close as she had been to her beloved Jerome!

"Thank *you* for saving my life Violette, I thought it was all over," Werner said and hugged her back, and then placed his lips against her forehead, as the rest of her face was already discoloured and swollen. He pushed her away just slightly to look into her face. "I don't know where we go from here, maybe it wasn't worth saving me. You can't stay here Violette, you must get back to the Cafe Marsaud. I will get one of my men to say that he drove you back to Café Marsaud, and Isabelle will back you up with that story. You must try to get your face looking better in case anyone sees you all beaten and bloodied." Werner said, and there was a deep ache in his chest as he wondered what would happen to this brave girl, who seemed to be unaware of her state of undress, and that the Chateau was filled with Gestapo Officers, who might well be keen to avenge the death of one of their colleagues.

"I could go away for a day or two maybe, until it looks better." Sarah said thoughtfully. "What will you do Werner, the Gestapo won't stop until they have found someone to pay for killing one of their men?"

"You are correct Violette, they will want vengeance, although he was in the wrong, and tried to kill me and he was killed in self defence. It won't make any difference to them." He walked around the room deep in thought, his hand pressed against the painful wound in the side of his chest, and he listened at the door, and everything seemed quiet. "Violette, you must go home now, you will have to put that dress on, and get home as quickly as you can. First can you help me lift Schiller's body onto the bed, we will cover him and maybe he won't be discovered until the morning. They will expect him to be hung-over anyway. That will give me time to think."

Schiller was a big man, and it took a great effort to get him onto the bed, and when it was done Werner pulled the knife out of his back, and replaced it with Schiller's own knife. He poured some water over the bloodied knife and looked across at Violette, and shrugged. He was surprised that she carried a knife, and he had never seen a knife exactly like that before. She had used that knife to save *his* life, and he really liked her, he would think about things in the morning, it worried him slightly that she had stabbed Schiller in exactly the right place. It could still have been a lucky strike as she had been in turmoil, trying to save her own and his life!

Werner held his hand against the badly aching wound in his side, as he watched as Violette pulled on the wine coloured dress, she seemed to be automatically dressing herself, and he wondered when the full meaning of what had happened would hit her, the side of her face was starting to swell and must hurt like hell, but she finished dressing herself.

CHAPTER THIRTEEN

Werner handed the washed knife back to Violette, and without thinking she found the strap lifted her skirt, and strapped it to her thigh. He watched thoughtfully, she was a beautiful woman and he was really drawn to her, not sexually, but as a friend he would have treasured in another time. He suddenly realised that she did excite him, and had he not been a married man, then he would have made a point of getting to know her. He realised that she would have to hide away for a day or two, as her face would be a mess, but first they must get her *out* of the Chateau, but she now looked strong and in control, the adrenalin must still be coursing through her veins. He thought he knew her and was sure that when she had gone over everything in her mind she would be devastated, but at least for now she was managing, and he was pleased to have been able to help her, even with the aching stab wound in his chest!

He didn't feel too good himself, the side of his chest hurt badly, but this wonderful girl had saved his life, just as he would not have allowed her to be violated, he would not do anything to endanger her life.

123

"Violette, I will lock the door from the inside. We will both go through the French windows onto the balcony. We will have to climb across to the next balcony it will not be easy, but probably easier than everything else we have already been through tonight," he moved to the French doors and they were not locked, probably because they were on the third floor of the Chateau. "From that room we will go out onto the landing, and then you will go down the servant's staircase and home, and I will go to my room. It will take you a while to walk home, but I had better stay around here, just in case something kicks off. All is quiet now, and should be for the rest of the night."

Sarah nodded, and suddenly he pulled her into his arms and they clung together for a moment. It seemed to give her strength, and he had renewed her belief in human nature, which had been sadly lacking during this long evening in which she had seen two dead bodies in desperate circumstances. For now she had to block out of her mind what she had seen and done, she must not put her French family in danger, but the full horror of it would haunt her for the rest of her life, however long or short that might be!

They managed the balconies by each helping the other - in particular he had to hold up her wine coloured dress as she stepped bravely from one balcony railing to the other, and she waited on the balcony to help him across. Surprisingly, they also cleared the bedroom next door, where there was a sleeping Gestapo man in the bed snoring loudly. Isabelle was nowhere to be seen, and Sarah was very pleased, as she had not wanted the older women to be involved in any way, in the only way she could Isabelle had done her best to help and advise Violette. She was also thankful that Marianne had not put in an appearance tonight.

Sarah was not seen or saw anyone else, on the large landing, and on her way down the servant's stairs through the kitchens, and the unlocked servant's door.

She reached the woods outside the Chateau grounds, and had to stop for a few minutes rest. She sat with her back against a tree, and she sobbed until she felt better and able to carry on. She truly hoped that Werner would not be in trouble, as he had only tried to help her – she knew Schiller would have raped her, and more than likely killed her. There was a War on, and the fact that there were two bodies unexpectedly found in Verneuil in one night, would hardly be noticed in the full scheme of things! Every death was a tragedy, and they could have included those of Werner Muller and Sarah Kate Graham!

When she arrived back at the Cafe Marsaud she was exhausted, and went around the back, and she then threw stones up at Gerrard's window. She thought she was going to have to sit outside all night, because she didn't see anything. She was shocked when Gerrard walked around from the back door without bringing any light at all, and he pulled her into his arms and hugged her, he had been living in dread at the thought of her turning up as yet another lost soul. She gave a little mew, as she was very sore from her fight with Schiller, and he lifted her up and carried her in by the back door of the Cafe, and carried on up to her bedroom. He gently placed her on the bed, at a loss as to how best to handle this young woman who was now like close family.

"Can you manage in the dark Violette, I dare not get a light," Gerrard whispered, wondering what had happened to her, but relieved that she was safely home. He thought of the body of the old Frenchman by the riverbank, if he had not been informed of that horrible discovery, he would not have missed Violette, he would have thought she was tucked up safely in her bed, what had she been through?

125

"I want to be alone Gerrard. I will have to talk to you when it comes light, leave it until then please." He could not ignore her heart-wrenching plea.

Gerrard moved away and closed her bedroom door, but he could still hear her crying quietly, and he was dreading what she had to tell him. Maybe it would be better if she told his mother, she was so heartbreakingly traumatised!

It was a couple of hours before Sarah managed to get any sleep, and she was still asleep when Madame Marsaud came into her room carrying a lamp, which she placed on a small bedside table. The old woman stared at Sarah's swollen and bruised face, and crossed herself, and rushed out to fetch her son from the Bakery.

Sarah awoke slowly with a groan, to find two worried faces staring down at her. She sat up quickly, and was carefully pressed back onto the bed by Madame Marsaud, her lined face so worried that Sarah tried to pull herself together.

"I will fetch the doctor," Gerrard said angrily. "Who did this to you, I'll kill him."

The right side of Sarah's face was very swollen and it made it difficult to speak. "No Gerrard, no doctor. And you don't need to kill him Gerrard, *I did*." Sarah said hopelessly, and sat up and tried to put her head in her hands, but it was too painful. She swung her legs to the floor, and realised she was still wearing the wine coloured dress. The colour was suitable, as it might well be smeared with blood! Blood from the man she had killed in defence of his intended victim, or from the one who had saved her from further harm!

Gerrard was dumbfounded, as was his mother. She had killed someone and had admitted it! She was not boasting about it or particularly regretful. It seemed it had been the only thing that she could do - a matter of her life or death!

126

As he thought of the reason she was here at all, he realised that it would be just as well if he and his mother were left to surmise, as it was much safer for everyone if they didn't know all of the sordid details.

Sarah knew she had to explain herself, and she must do it quickly before anyone came to the cafe, most likely from the Chateau Genevieve! Werner had stressed that she should keep herself out of sight, at least until her obviously battered face had improved in appearance, and then she wondered if it would be better if she made her way to the coast as she had on her last visit to France, safer for herself and her adopted French family.

"I had been to the boathouse to use the wireless, and when I was leaving I found a body, it was almost the worst experience of my life." Gerrard and Madame glanced at each other knowingly. "At the bridge I was abducted by Oberleutnant Heinrich Schiller, who I think killed the old man, and was taken to the Chateau. I was made to dress up in that dress, which I'd like you to burn Aunt Bridgette, and forced to stay at the Chateau. After dinner Schiller took me to his room. We fought, and he was going to kill me, when someone pulled him off me, and they fought, and Schiller tried to kill him with his knife, and before he could stab the man a second time, I finished Schiller off with my knife. I owe that man my life." Tears were running down her face, and she knew she had to pull herself together, or they would all be in danger.

"You are a heroine Violette, you did well, I wish we could tell the family of the old man who was killed, but we can't, although it must have been Heinrich Schiller," Madame remarked with chagrin.

"I must keep out of sight until my face is better. Or better still we should try to contact Jean Distelle to arrange for me to move away from here, I am becoming a danger to your

127

family, and the Resistance. Too many people know that I was at the Chateau, although under duress."

"I will talk with Jean and let you know. For now you should hide in the loft, I don't think they would bother searching that again. As far as anyone is concerned you have gone home to stay with your mother for a few days." Gerrard decided. "I must get back to the bakery, and make everything seem as normal."

"I will burn that dress, and bring you something to bathe your face. Stay in your room and only go up in the loft if you hear anything out of the ordinary." Madame said, and Sarah started to wash and dress as best she could.

She kept seeing the old man and his grotesque death mask - he had not deserved to die. He was most likely someone's grandfather, and it brought home to her that that was why she was here, to try to prevent these things happening across the channel! Almost as frightening had been the hate-filled face of Schiller after she had attempted to stab him in the eyes with her fingers. She felt very sick, and had to take some deep breaths, to enable her to carry on.

She finished dressing, and bathed her face with water, and patted it with witch-hazel, just as there was a loud banging on the door of the Cafe. Sarah ached considerably as she moved into the landing area, and placed her foot on top of the low chest of drawers, ready to haul herself upwards through the trapdoor. Every part of her body ached and she knew if she managed it, it would be through sheer necessity.

"It's alright Violette, a young soldier just left a note for you, also one for me," Gerrard said in surprise. He was reading his as he came up the stairs, and suddenly smiled. "It's from Oberst Werner Muller, he says 'thank you for the coffee and croissants over the last few months, and he has now been called away to the front line." He handed a note to

Violette. "As German's go he was alright." He hurried back down the stairs as it was now time to open the bakery and cafe. He also wanted to see Monsieur Jean Distelle, or Jacques Flamand if they came into the bakery. They both had to be warned that things might be very unpleasant in the next few days.

Sarah read Werner's note with tears in her eyes, she would miss seeing him in the cafe where he had enjoyed his coffee and croissants most mornings. He had proved himself to be a true friend, and she hoped that she had not put him in danger. She hoped that what he said in his note was the truth, and that in due course he would be reunited with his wife and daughters. Later she burned the note over a candle.

Three days later Violette was again helping in the bakery and cafe, with make-up covering her still bruised face, and as she had thought she really did miss Werner Muller very much, and she was anxious on his behalf, and hoped that he had managed to get away as he had intended.

The next morning an armoured car arrived at the Bakery, with a request that she should come to the Chateau immediately.

She had expected some sort of inquiry would be made regarding the death of Heinrich Schiller, and she was driven to the Chateau in a state of agitation, and strived with her whole body to betray no emotion when she saw who was awaiting her. It was Wilhelm Schmidt, whom she noticed had been promoted to Oberleutnant (First Officer) from Leutnant (Second Officer) – it appeared that he had *benefited* from the death of his colleague.

She was taken into a large room, with a very large desk at which a Gestapo Colonel asked her questions in halting French. She said that she had been driven home by one of the soldiers at the request of Oberst Muller. 'No,' she didn't know the man's name or rank, and 'no' she hadn't seen

Oberst Muller at the Chateau except on one occasion weeks ago. Also that she didn't really know, but Madame Isabelle Genevieve may have seen her leave, but she wasn't sure.

She was relieved and surprised that she was allowed to leave the Chateau, and she was escorted out of the room by Wilhelm Schmidt. He walked with her to the armoured car on the drive, and opened the door for her. Suddenly as he bent down towards her, he hissed menacingly in her ear, "You did well in the Inquiry Mademoiselle, but *I* didn't believe a word of it, and you must not think you have won. You will be under *my* surveillance." He stood back and watched the car move along the driveway to the gateway of the Chateau. He knew in his gut that she was involved with the killing of Schiller, and thought that she and her family, Madame and Gerrard Marsaud should be punished. He would wait until the time was right, then he would act to avenge the death of that pompous ass Schiller, who had given him such a hard time in the past!

There had been a lot of gossip about what had happened at the Chateau the night that Oberleutnant Heinrich Schiller had been killed. Some said that he had been killed with his own knife, and it was an accident. Others said that he had very few friends, and had made enemies with some of his Gestapo colleagues. However, none of the townspeople ever did find out exactly the result of the Inquiry, it was a military matter, and the army of occupation would deal with it.

Jean Distelle, having learned from Gerrard part of what had happened, had apparently contacted London, and it had been decided that Violette should have recovery time, and for the time being no further action would be taken by the Resistance, neither would any contact be made with London for a considerable time. The occupying Germans must be lulled into a false sense of security.

CHAPTER FOURTEEN

Evan John had been promoted to a Flying Officer, and Jerome had been made a Squadron Leader, but they had both been flying none stop for weeks it seemed. They were busily occupied and the time seemed to fly as quickly as their aeroplane, except through the nights when Jerome realised that instead of weeks, his wife had been away for months and months on end. Evan in every quiet moment tried to connect with his twin, but he was always disappointed.

Evan had a few days off and was intent on going home to the Lake District for rest and recuperation with his family. They were in The Royal Oak, and Jerome seemed really pissed off, and Evan couldn't remember a time when has been so low in spirits.

Jerome also had a few days leave, and intended as usual, to make a nuisance of himself at the 'big house' where both he and Evan knew that Sarah Kate had been living. If anyone knew where she was, then they were in that building. All he wanted to know was that she was safe and well, not what she was doing or where she was! They were both really angry now that they realised that Sarah Kate's Commanding

131

Officer had sent her on her way without letting her know that her husband had, in fact, been thrown clear of his burning aircraft and had survived! Evan particularly wondered if she might take unnecessary risks, risks that she wouldn't take if she knew she had her husband waiting for her return, and as time went on and the War seemed to escalate he began to doubt that either *he* or *Jerome* would be around for his sister!

****

Jerome had been upset since early morning, as he had been once again turned away and threatened with the red caps, which would not be the first time. However, the man he had spoken to through the door, as he wasn't allowed in, had lost his rag a bit and said "Go away Squadron Leader, *nobody* knows exactly where you wife is." His brooding deliberations were again interrupted by Evan.

"Jerome, remember when you and Sarah Kate married you intended to go up and visit the family. You didn't have time, and spent a couple of days in Wales for a honeymoon. Why don't you come home with me now it will be a complete change, and you will see where Sarah Kate and I spent our childhood, and you will get to know more about her, her likes and dislikes, what she liked to do before she met you, all sorts of things." He paused, his mind in a whirl wondering how to help his brother-in-law. Jerome needed something to occupy him, and get his mind onto other things if only for a brief length of time!

"Besides it will help me, I usually get questioned all the time by the evacuees, our cousins and family - you could take some of the flack."

"Oh I don't know Evan, as they will be busy and excited seeing you again, without bothering with a stranger." Jerome replied, his mind toying with Evan's surprise invitation, Sarah Kate had often mentioned the valley, and how she loved it.

"You are not a stranger Jerome. They know that you looked after Sarah Kate when I was missing, they'll want to thank you for that at least."

Jerome thought about it, and glanced across at Evan. "If I come I don't think we should say that I'm their son-in-law, they might not approve of a pilot as a husband for their elder daughter. They could think we did it just because I'm a flyer, but it was much more than that Evan. Sarah Kate and I intend to spend the rest of our lives together, however long or short that may be. I guess it wouldn't hurt to visit your family, and it just might help keep me sane. Every now and then I feel like blowing my top, and it would be with those people in the place where Sarah was living, I might be better somewhere else even for a few days."

On the journey up to the Lakes, and from Windermere Station to the valley, Jerome was very impressed by the countryside, particularly the last thirty miles or so. He said it was like Canada, but more compact, but just as grand in its own way. He also said that as soon as the War was over, he hoped to go back to Canada and take his wife with him to meet his parents. He knew they would love her, as did he.

They arrived at Rowan Trees, and as soon as the door was opened Jerome thought it was all a bit chaotic, when a young woman, obviously Sarah Kate's sister, threw herself into Evan's arms. Declaring that after nearly two years she was fit and well, she no longer had tuberculosis, and the family were celebrating that fact.

There was also more good news, their cousin Harold Birkett and his uncle Charlie Jones were back in the valley, and when Jerome was introduced they all had a good talk about the War, some of it quite subdued. However, after a while Jerome was properly introduced to Evan and Sarah, his wife's parents, and he liked them very much, and thought that they liked him, although to them he was just a friend of Evan John. Jerome liked the characteristics that he realised had come from either Evan or Sarah to their twins, and he liked them all. He also liked Megs and wondered if Sarah Kate would have been as ebullient and happy as her sister in different circumstances.

They enjoyed a welcoming meal, and it seemed a little awkward when Evan John offered Jerome a cigarette, but Evan John's mother said she didn't mind them smoking, her husband liked a pipe now and then. However, Jerome looked at young Megs face, and she was very disapproving, as well she might having just spent nearly two years recovering from tuberculosis, apparently contacted briefly as a land girl.

When Evan and Sarah Evans thanked Jerome for looking after their daughter whilst Evan was listed as 'missing,' Jerome couldn't stand it any more and told them he didn't just look after Sarah Kate, he loved her, and she was his soul-mate and his wife. And in almost the same breath he told them he didn't know where she was!

His in-laws looked really shocked, and Megs seemed kind of relieved, as if she knew that *both* Evan John and Jerome were looking out for Sarah Kate. Megs also realised that things might change somewhat, as Jerome Graham was now Sarah Kate's next of kin. She glanced at her parents, and realised that they seemed to like Jerome, it just seemed to have flummoxed them somewhat, that neither Jerome nor Evan John, knew where their daughter was! She was aware that her dad had surmised a long time ago, when they received letters from Sarah Kate, which seemed all wrong, that she was something else besides a Code and Cipher Officer! And Megs had listened to Evan John at one time when he was worried about his twin, and needed to talk to someone.

Megs heard the low voices of Jerome, Evan and her dad talking long into the night – eventually she slept and dreamt of her sister and strangely, Zeke Williams, and they were still at school including herself sitting in her pram!

Two evenings later, it was a dark, foggy night, and a lot of the villagers were out on the village green, listening with dread as a plane (a Halifax both Jerome and Evan agreed) droned around the valley obviously looking for a way out. It was with consternation that they eventually heard a loud bang which reverberated around the valley like a quarry blast, and a strange light could be seen for a few minutes high on the mountains at the head of the valley, followed by an ominous deathly silence.

Jerome was impressed by the speed and efficiency of Evan Evans, his son Evan, and most of the younger men in the valley, as they all converged on Rowan Trees without being asked, and soon they were leaving the valley in the quarry truck to drive to the next valley, which was the nearest point to the expected crash site. Jerome joined them, and Evan John informed him that his dad was the leader of any rescues on the fells, and also the Home Guard, and as most of the men did both, they were now used to working together, which was good for anyone needing their help!

That night was to remain in Jerome's mind for the rest of his life, as he was particularly upset as the crew were all Canadians, and there were no survivors. Jerome was also amazed when Megs Evans and her cousin arrived with rucksacks full of hot drinks and food for the men, who would wait at the site during the night. The doctor and the vicar both arrived together.

There was nothing that could be done, except that the site was protected until the RAF could get there within the next few days.

Jerome and Evan talked together seriously, and Evan John assured his sister's husband, that as her twin he thought she was still alive, and they set off back to their RAF Base, determined to try to find her. The weeks that Sarah Kate had informed Evan that she would be away, would soon be years. It felt like decades as far as Jerome was concerned. He looked at his healed burns, which to him seemed to be quite minor, and wondered if she would ever see them, and what would she think if she did. He was obviously damaged on the outside, and he felt like screaming inside. He coaxed his tense muscles to relax, and tried to appear calm - it might be a while before he saw her.

CHAPTER FIFTEEN

Life at the Cafe Marsaud had drifted into a satisfactory routine. As indeed it should, as for the moment the Resistance was resting in order to get the Gestapo and SS Troops at the Chateau to fall into a false sense of security. No communications had been made with London for months.

Much as Sarah had slipped into family mode with Madame Marsaud and her son Gerrard, she longed to return home, or get on with what she had been sent to France to do!

However, there was one particular fly in her ointment, namely Oberleutnant Wilhelm Schmidt.

Upon occasions he now came into the cafe for coffee with one or two colleagues, and as soon as they arrived the place went silent, and the few French customers usually drifted away silently. Schmidt also noticed that Violette was never alone in the cafe, there was always Gerrard, or at times a very large French woman who was quite formidable even for the Gestapo, who had been told not to antagonise the locals at least until the officer who had come in to do the Inquiry regarding the death of Schiller had returned to his

137

trouble shooting job. The poor man was anxious to leave, but had been told to stay to keep relationships with the locals at the very least reasonably quiet, no confrontations were to occur!

Wilhelm had been pleased with his promotion after the death of Heinrich Schiller. However, since the death of Heinrich Schiller the Gestapo Commanding Officer had been quite strict, making sure that the rules of the Armistice Agreement signed by Hitler were followed to the letter (for the time being) and those rules were most certainly to the advantage of the Germans. The dinners at the Chateau were still frequented by the ladies of questionable virtue, but so far no more young local women had been forced to attend.

Jean Distelle and the other Resistance members were well aware that since the death of Schiller, the Gestapo had made more frequent patrols around the town, and there were many more Gestapo officers keeping a high profile in the area. When they did resume their work, then it would not be as easy with the extra Gestapo presence, and most likely, more dangerous than before!

Sarah during the day felt she was coping very well. However, during the night when sleeping she had no control over her emotions, and was subject to nightmares in which she frequently saw the body of the old Frenchman with his grotesque death mask, and that of Schiller in his masochistic lustful rage. These nightmares frequently left her tired and lethargic the next day. Madame Marsaud obviously slept very well, as she only twice came in to Violette's room to see what was bothering her.

Sarah was surprised when Jean Distelle came to the cafe, as he had not been seen in the area for a while, and as usual when he paid for his buns, he left her a note.

She retired to the bakery, and read the note. Jean had requested a meeting at the old boathouse on the river this evening. Later she walked along the path alongside the river, and it brought back to her the death of the old man. She was both frightened and angry, and hoped that Jean had something for her to do to help the locals extract some sort of vengeance for his terrible death. She pushed open the door cautiously, and recognised the silhouettes of Jean Distelle, and Jacques Flamand.

Jean she had seen earlier today, but she kissed Jacques on both cheeks as she had not seen him for a long time.

"Is Marianne well," she asked, deciding not to mention the fact that she had seen his sister at the Chateau, just in case he didn't know anything about her being there! Jacques seemed weak and thin and she realised that he had not, nor was he likely to recover from the beating he had received by the Gestapo.

"She is well, and looking forward to seeing you," Jacques said quietly.

"Violette, I have spoken with London. They know about Oberleutnant Schmidt, and the fact that he is still watching you. More often than you know Violette as *we* have been watching *him*," Jean said warningly. "Therefore, you are to go and stay with your 'mother' that is, Madame Marsaud, who lives the other side of Sainte Pierre. Madame Marsaud's home, since the death of her daughter, has become a safe house for escaping prisoners of war, this is important work as it boosts the moral of other prisoners to hear of any success, and it upsets the Germans. Madame Marsaud is unwell, and cannot guide them to the next safe house. So as your mother is ill, you are leaving to look after her, as far as anyone in Verneuil is concerned. When Schmidt is moved on, and your 'mother' is better then you can return to Verneuil and your cousin's bakery, and we can start to create havoc once again for the occupying Germans! My mother is staying with Madame Marsaud, but since the death of my father she keeps a low profile, and you will not see much of her, as unfortunately, neither do I." Jean said sadly, but seemed quite excited by the prospect of starting some further work with the Resistance in the not too distant future.

"Good, I am ready to do anything, the last few weeks have seemed like a life sentence," Violette said briskly. "What about 'Violette's' mother, how will she react to having her dead daughter's stand-in living in her home, she might resent the fact that her daughter is dead and I am alive, it could be very difficult for her?"

"As you are aware, she has done everything that she can to make the lives of the Germans as difficult as possible, hence the safe house." Jean said, looking closely at Violette. "Schmidt is a danger to you. You are tired, and have been suffering from nightmares, we are aware of this," he said as she tried to interrupt him. "We have been told to move you away, there is no way that they can come and fly you out at the moment, this is the best option, and you will be available when we need you."

"Very well Jean I guess I don't have an option, but how will I travel to Sainte Pierre and then to the home of Gerrards' aunt, by bus?" Sarah asked, thinking that she would at least be doing something useful.

"Yes, by bus to Sainte Pierre, and then Marianne will have a bicycle ready for you and instructions for the rest of your journey," Jean replied.

"Oh Jean, did the Resistance find the sleeve gun that I hid in the grass, when Schiller abducted me?" A few days after her confrontation with Schiller, she had remembered the sleeve gun, and had been worried about someone finding it, as it could have been very dangerous.

"Yes they did, but it had been there for days in bad weather, and it didn't look very safe, it is in the bottom of the river now. If you were to try to use it now, it might kill you." Jacques answered with a rueful smile. "Marianne will be ready for you from noon tomorrow." He smiled at Violette, and she smiled back in agreement.

Sarah solemnly shook hands with them both, and then Jean kissed her on the forehead. "Don't forget Violette, you must not contact me or the cafe, I will contact you when the time is right."

She left the boathouse, and it took all her resolve to walk along the river path, instead of running as fast as she could. Maybe they were correct, maybe she needed a rest from this place, and from any chance of meeting Schmidt.

As she packed her belongings the next morning, she was tempted to take the wireless which was still hidden in the loft of the Cafe, she didn't think it would be used unless Jean Distelle had a need of it in the near future. However, he had instructed her that he would be in touch with her and not for her to contact him.

The bus journey was much as the one she had taken to Verneil from Sainte Pierre, but she felt a bit more relaxed, knowing that she would be meeting Marianne. She remembered that on her first visit to Verneuil she had not even known the whereabouts of the Cafe Marsaud, and remembered that Werner Muller had escorted her there. She truly hoped that Werner was alright, and was not being pursued for the alleged murder of Schiller!

Marianne was waiting sitting casually on the steps of the cottage where Sarah had spent a night many months ago. She walked around the corner of the house and brought back with her a bicycle, again with a basket on the front, filled with provisions. She handed Violette the handlebars, and placed her forefinger on the end of the metal, indicating that the instructions were hidden inside, under the handgrip.

"Follow the road out of the village to the right, and when you come to a bridge, you should be safe to read the

141

instructions. Good luck Violette." Marianne appeared to be sympathising with her, and Sarah wondered if she was aware of why she was being sent away from Verneuil, and what had happened at the Chateau.

At the bridge Sarah read the instructions, and followed the path to a farm which seemed to be miles from anywhere. She went to the door and knocked, dreading this meeting with the mother of the real, but deceased, Violette Marsaud. She glanced around the farmyard, and the only person she could see was an elderly man working near the barn. The property seemed rather run down, but then all the men had been away fighting, and not many had managed to return to their homes since the Armistice with Hitler in June 1940, which seemed a long time ago. She thought again, it was nearly four years ago!

The door opened and a woman with white hair and a much younger face, wearing a long black dress and a stained apron, stared back at Sarah. She put her hand to her chest and breathed very hard and long.

"Gerrard did try to warn me that you looked like *my* Violette. Perhaps when you are here at the farm you would not wear plaits, it makes my heart jerk, and then I am disappointed when I realise you are not my Violette. I am sorry you are doing a very good job I believe, thank you." Madame Marsaud stood aside and indicated that Sarah should move into the house. The hallway led to a working kitchen, which looked to Sarah as if it could do with a thorough clean. She couldn't blame the bereaved women beside her, her life must feel like it was over since the death of her daughter, yet she was finding the energy and time to assist escaped prisoners of war. "I understand Violette (I will call you Violette) that you need to be away from Verneuil for the time being. I need your help, I cannot move as easily as I could and there is no-one here except me, old Will, and

Jean's mother. Old Will, you will have seen in the yard. Later, I will show you the way to the next safe house. Any escapees usually only stay a couple of days, they need to keep moving as much as possible. You must rest for a while Violette, your room is at the top of the stairs, turn left." Madame Marsaud said, "but bring in your things from the bike, before we have any callers, who believe me are few and far between."

Sarah brought her things into the house, and made up the bed, and made her room ready. She then helped Madame Marsaud in the kitchen, and Will came into the house for a meal. He didn't say anything at all, but seemed to understand what was said to him. Madame Distelle was taken a small tray to her room. Sarah watched Old Will as he ate, and realised that one hand was very weak, and his lips seemed to sag at one side. She glanced at Madame Marsaud, and she nodded briefly, it appeared that Will had suffered a stroke at some time.

The next day early, Madame Marsaud awoke Sarah, and they trudged off across the countryside for about an hour, through a large wood, and down another valley, and then from a high point she indicated a farmstead in the distance, with a thickly forested area behind it. "See the farmhouse, well there is a small shack in the forest behind it. That is where you will send anyone who passes through. If they stick to the stream in the bottom of the valley, there are plenty of places to hide, should anyone travel along the cart track below us. Sometimes we get people with us for a couple of days or even more, but they must move on as quickly as possible, and you should not get too involved with them, or let them know anything about you." She finished adamantly.

"Do they stay with us in the house?" Sarah asked.

"No, nor in the barn, both the house and barn are searched if any Germans passing come searching. They are hidden behind the pig sty, which is not cleaned out very often by Will. However, they usually eat in the house," Madame Marsaud smiled and shrugged. "We haven't had any discovered yet."

Two lazy days, except for cleaning the house, passed before anything happened. Sarah was becoming quite settled and relaxed. Without warning two German cars arrived in the farmyard, and noisily and with guns ready, the six soldiers searched the farmhouse and the barn, and the surrounding fields. They found nothing, but it was not very pleasant, and Sarah was quite shaken up when they at last left, after scrutinizing her papers. They had obviously been here before, and although her papers were authentic she had been very apprehensive. It wasn't until after they had left the property, that she wondered if they had any connection with Verneuil, and the Chateau Genevieve where the name of Violette Marsaud could at some time have been mentioned!

The next day Madame Marsaud asked Sarah to go to the bridge at which she had read the instructions to the farm provided by Marianne. She was to wait there, and she would be met, and from there she would bring someone to the farm, and the next day she would take them on to the area she had been shown by Madame Marsaud.

Sarah waited on the bridge, and after a while a girl on a bicycle stopped, and asked if she was Violette Marsaud. Sarah nodded, and the girl told her that the package she was awaiting was under the bridge, and she rode off in the direction of Sainte Pierre. After a couple of minutes when all was silent except for birdsong, and the humming of a bee, she moved down under the bridge.

In front of her was a young man crouching beside the river. He was dressed in civilian country style clothes, but he

144

looked very little more than a boy. She asked him in French if he spoke that language. He did a little he said, so she thought she would stick to French. The less they knew about each other the better. She indicated that he should follow, and without incident they arrived at the Farm Marsaud. He was fed in the kitchen, taken to wash in the yard at the back, and given a blanket, a small bottle of home made wine, a paper bag of food, and taken to the pig sty by the silent Will, who smiled at him reassuringly, and hid him away. However, there was a secret door that he could open and close himself which opened away from the pig sty and looked over a ploughed field.

Violette watched him as he settled in and she was amazed at how calm and self assured he seemed for one so young. She did realise that he must have fought, been captured and then escaped to be here at all, and she prayed that he would make it back home, and she would have loved to talk with him but Madame had said she must not become too involved or know too much. Maybe Madame was correct, she had much more experience in these matters than Sarah.

Later in bed with moonlight spilling across the room, Sarah wondered about the young man once again. His accent had been Scottish, and she longed to go and speak to him, he was so young and must feel terribly lonely, as she did herself. She missed her family and Evan John, and Jerome so much that it hurt her chest. She was soon in tears, and realised that if she had gone to speak to the young man she would have been in a much worse state than she was just thinking about him. He could well have felt the same meeting someone who had been born just sixty miles away from his home! Madame was quite correct, she must stay aloof if she possibly could. She wiped away the tears, and went to sleep thinking of Jerome's brown expressive eyes.

She sighed thankfully she could still remember his eyes, but she longed to feel his arms around her, and feel the comfort and bliss that had given her! She must think of Evan John and try to believe that he was still safe and well and keeping in touch with their parents and Megs.

CHAPTER SIXTEEN

Sarah made another mistake the next day. After he had eaten a good breakfast, and washed, she escorted the young Scotsman through the woods, down the valley, and to the high place where the next farm was visible. It had been difficult to keep from chattering away to him, asking questions about where he was from and about his escape!

He thanked her profusely for her help, and sustenance, and she smiled and shook his hand. He held on to her hand, and she suddenly pulled him close with her arms around him, he looked so alone. He held on tight, and she tried to push him away but he was crying, and spoke partly in English.

"You remind me of my mother and sister, I'm trying to get back to them, and my unit will probably send me straight back to fight." He sounded so hopeless.

She gently moved him away from her, and tapped the side of her nose with her forefinger. "A little bird told me that the Allies are doing well in North Africa, the Far East and Europe. Just think of your mother and sister, they will be so proud of you when you get back. So will the men you

147

have left behind, you are doing it for them too, and bonny Scotland." She said bracingly in French. Then she showed him the countryside and told him where he must be before nightfall, giving him time to pull himself together. He looked surprised, then pleased, and she realised she had spoken in French and he had understood, but 'A little bird told me' and 'bonny Scotland' did not have much of a French ring to it! "You must get there before nightfall," she reminded him in the language which had become second nature to her. He smiled, braced himself and slid down the banking, and she watched until he was under cover of the trees that grew beside the stream and he was out of her sight.

A few weeks later the Marsaud farm now looked spick and span and she hadn't anything to occupy her except helping Madame and Will with the house and farmyard. All the farm land was now farmed by farmer neighbours, who seemed few and far between!

She had been the guide for six other prisoners of war, two more single ones and a couple of pairs. She had been quite reserved as she had been warned by Madame Marsaud, except for one of the prisoners who was travelling alone. He had not changed his clothes into local rural, but was still wearing flying boots, and before she had realised it she had asked if he was RAF. He had not told her yes or no, but had looked down at his flying boots knowing that they had given him away. He was wary of her as he should be and she had not spoken again of anything, other than giving him instructions for the next part of his journey.

When last she had spoken to Jean Distelle the little information she had imparted to the Scotsman had been correct as far as she knew, but since then she had been completely cut off from any knowledge of the War situation. She decided to give Jean a few more days and if she didn't hear anything, then she was going back into Sainte Pierre on her bicycle to try to find Marianne. Surely she or Jacques would know something of what was going on in the War, or even something about the Resistance, as Sarah could not believe that they had desisted from being a thorn in the side of the Germans occupying their country!

The Germans who had come and searched the farm had not been back, and she started to believe that she would not be a threat to the local French population. It looked as if the Gestapo at Chateau Genevieve had believed that she had nothing to do with the death of Oberleutnant Heinrich Schiller. That must be very old news now.

During the next four weeks, Sarah went to the bridge at regular intervals as normal, but there were no prisoners of war, or anyone wanting to use the safe house route out of France. Sarah needed something to fill in her time, she was brooding and wanted to see her family, and she was pining just as much as ever for her husband. The people who said it would get better with time, did not know what they were talking about!

Madame seemed very well as far as Sarah could ascertain, and if Sarah was to have no part in the Resistance, then she might as well make use of the safe houses, and make her way back to the coast and home, she had done that quite successfully before. She still had the papers of Violette Marsaud which were completely authentic, and her trusty knife, which she only strapped to her thigh when doing her escort work, or when she was out of the farmhouse.

The days were hot and sunny and she had a tendency to restlessness, and she began to feel superfluous which was hard to bear. There was no sign of Jean Distelle or Marianne Flamand, as another young women from Sainte Pierre was now bringing the prisoners of war as far as the bridge, and these were very few and far between, and now Sarah had taken to waiting under the bridge every third day, sometimes she had someone to escort, sometimes not, but there was no need to make any contact between the farm and Sainte Pierre. What she was doing was easy and well planned, and Madame could quite easily do it herself.

"Madame I'm going to ride into Sainte Pierre today, I need to make contact with Marianne or Jacques. I thought Jean Distelle would have been in touch before now, he must know what is going on, and I can't stay here forever, and you would think he would at least visit his mother. Can you manage to do the necessary guide work?"

"I always could Violette, Jean wanted you out of Verneuil for your own safety, and theirs of course. The Resistance and the Marsaud family all thank you for what you have done. They still have the wireless sets and I think they must once again be in contact with London."

"In that case Madame, if I can't contact Jean or Marianne, then I might as well follow the route of the prisoners of war, or try to get home by bus, train and fishing boat, as I did once before." Sarah thought she sounded quite petty, but she was a bit upset, she obviously wasn't needed around here now. Or had the French suddenly given up all thoughts of causing a nuisance to the Germans? She felt rather stupid, and went to her room and shed a few tears. She wanted to see her family, she missed them so much, and she needed something to occupy her, she was aware that she spent her time pining for Jerome, and that wasn't very healthy, even she knew that!

Her trip into Sainte Pierre was uneventful and a pleasant change to her usual routine, and she called at the house at which she had stayed with Marianne and Jacques, but nobody came to the house in the time she waited. As she didn't see Marianne or Jacques, she could not, therefore, contact Jean. There was a little farmer's market, and she decided to buy some provisions, it would look better if she returned to the farm with some shopping. She decided to return to the Marsaud farm and talk over her plans with Madame, who could inform the Resistance of Violette's plans in due course, whenever either Marianne and Jacques, or Jean made the effort to make contact.

Sarah felt slightly more relaxed as she climbed on her bicycle for the return journey. It had been good to get away from the farm for an hour or so, and she thought of seeing Evan John, her parents, her extended family all three generations, and regaling Megs with all of her exploits over these few years. Well, not all of them, besides she was forgetting, her trainer's and CO had made quite a thing about signing the Official Secrets Act! She smiled to herself remembering her young sister Megs, who had always been very busy writing in her journals, and doing articles for the Westmorland Gazette the local paper. At least she had, until she had contacted tuberculosis, and it had been a shock to learn that she was in a Sanatorium – I hope you are getting well again Megs, she whispered and hoped that Meg's Guardian Angel was listening. She looked at the fruit in the basket in front of her bicycle, and thought that maybe she could manage a bite or two of one of those golden delicious apples. She took a bite and quickly dropped the apple back in the basket. A car was coming behind her, and didn't seem to be slowing down - then the engine did slow, and she carried on whereas she had been thinking of going into the side of the road and stopping. The vehicle engine picked up again and at the last minute when it closed in on her, she looked angrily at the driver of the car, and looked straight into the cold eyes of Oberleutnant Wilhelm Schmidt – her heart jolted in her chest, his eyes reminded her of Heinrich Schiller, coldly hostile and deadly. She knew from his expression that she had been recognised, and she noticed there were two of them in the front of the armoured car. She started to peddle as fast as she could, if she could get to the narrow bridge he would have to slow down.

Her chest was thumping with the added exertion needed to move ahead of the car. She glanced back and noticed his determined grimace and his iron control as he turned the wheel with evil intent, to try to run into her bike and force her off the road. He had not noticed the bridge coming up and she suddenly braked, but the car hit her bike and she flew through the air, and luckily she landed in soft grass beside the river. However, she was winded and there a sharp pain in her side and lower chest, and she knew she had broken some ribs. She must be badly bruised all down one side, but she managed to move after a few minutes of trying desperately to get some air into her lungs. She slowly pulled herself into a standing position, all the while waiting for a heavy German hand to detain her. She stared in front of her in dismay.

The car driven by Wilhelm Schmidt had hit the bridge, rolled over and landed with the front wheels in the river, which was flowing quite fast. The two Germans were still and silent in the front of the car, and she dragged herself down the bank towards them. She opened the driver's door, and put her fingers to Wilhelm Schmidt's neck. His pulse was strong, and she assumed that he was just knocked out. She went quickly to the other side of the car, and again felt for a pulse in the other German's neck, it was beating. But he was in a strange ungainly position and she worried he would not be able to continue to breath, and she opened the door and pulled him out onto the grassy slope, and put him in on his side and he at least looked more comfortable.

Sarah struggled back to the mangled bicycle, and managed to get the basket off the front, and this she pulled across the road away from the river and hid it in the hedge. She then collected everything that had been thrown out of the basket, and returned it to the basket. She knew she must hurry, as Wilhelm and his colleague could regain consciousness at any time, but she felt rather dizzy and her chest ached abominably. She placed her bike on the road where it could plainly be seen, and wondered if they might think that she had been thrown into the river and swept away! Should she blow on the horn to get attention or not? It might bring help for the two men, but it might also arouse them, and she felt lousy as her chest was extremely painful, she had a headache, her forearm felt strangely numb, and she knew without any doubt that she wouldn't be able to get away.

She moved across the road to where she had hidden the basket of shopping from the market, and hauled herself and the basket up the slight rise. Luckily she was on the side of the road opposite to the Marsaud farm. She could not return to the farm, she was now on her own. The bad news was that she didn't know how badly she had been hurt, as she hurt all over. The good news was that she had the purchases made in Sainte Pierre to sustain her for a little while, and her trusty knife.

She waited in the wooded area about two hundred yards from the smashed car with its wheels in the river. She knew what she *should* do, she should have finished off the two men with her knife, or at least Schmidt who had recognised her, but she knew she could not kill again. She had killed Schiller in order to save a life, a better life than his, the life of a loving husband and father, but she would *never* do that again. She really believed she had done the right thing in that instance, but split-second decisions might not always be so. She still had nightmares about it, even though she realised that it was either Schiller or Werner Muller and there was no contest!

She also had to distance herself from the *accident* or she might be seen, but she had to make sure that the two men were found and helped, so she waited in considerable pain and very impatiently.

She saw movement and the passenger whom she had pulled out of the car, started to move, then slowly he pulled himself up beside the car. He checked on Wilhelm Schmidt, and then looked around the area, and she assumed he was looking for her body! He paused wondering which way to go, then he slowly limped his way towards the village of Sainte Pierre.

Sarah looked around her, and sighed, it would take her all day to pull herself up through the field to the wooded area, and thus find cover. She had not got a clue as to which way she should go, and realised that she only had what she was wearing, she really needed to go to the farm and collect some clothing, and the small amount of francs that she owned. Then her best plan was to try to get herself well, and miss out Madame Marsaud's farm, and try to follow the safe houses to the coast.

It took all of her courage to stay exactly where she was, able to see the tow truck, and German vehicles which came to the scene of the accident. Schmidt and his colleague were taken away by car, and a group of Germans after looking around the area, and seeing the Marsaud farmhouse in the distance, immediately went to do a search. As soon as they had left the area, Sarah tried to stand, but she had great difficulty, also she had difficulty in breathing and she wondered if a lung had been punctured by her ribs. It must have taken her about two hours to struggle towards the farm, as she had to keep stopping to rest. It was moonlight when she got there, with clouds obscuring the moon periodically. However, she noticed that the Mesdames Marsaud and Distelle, also Will had already retired for the night. They probably had assumed that she was staying with Marianne. She went in through the pantry window, which was very painful indeed, as it was quite a small window. From there she managed to get to her room, and collect her belongings. She wore as many clothes as she could, carried the rest in her small case, and was so tired she decided to spend a few hours in the place the prisoners of war hid, behind the pigsty. Before she went there she found some bread and cheese, and a wine bottle with a cork in which to carry drinking water.

Once able to relax in her hiding place, she used her knife to cut up a cotton underskirt into strips with which to bind her ribs, she smiled to herself ruefully as this was the last time she could do that, it was her last cotton underskirt!

She must have managed a couple of hours sleep, and then she was moving off to get as far away from the farm as she could before daylight. She was certain she was doing the right thing in not waking Madame Marsaud, if asked she could say truthfully that she had no idea where her *daughter* was! She tried to remember in which direction from the farm, she had been dropped by parachute into France, in relation to Sainte Pierre, and tried to work out from that a place to go to recover from her injuries.

For the next two days and nights she continued on her way, with short rests, all the while wondering if she should try to contact the Resistance, but she might only put them in danger if she asked for help. Was she a woman or a mouse, besides she had enough food with her to keep her going for a week or two if she was careful. All she needed was a chemist shop, for some painkillers, and then she would reach her destination where she could rest for as long as she needed, and give her painful body time to heal.

She found herself on the outskirts of Sainte Pierre at the side she had never been before. She pulled a scarf over her blonde hair, and put on her winter coat to cover her bandaged body, and then ventured into town to find a 'Pharmacie.' She saw her reflection in one of the shop windows and realised that she would not be recognised, as with her aches and pains she looked like a stooped and old woman, as she was wearing quite a lot of her clothes, as that was the easiest way to carry them. As for her face it was rather more bruised than she had expected.

She stopped in her tracks in the town and looked around. Everything seemed to be very light hearted. There were no Germans or German vehicles around, and some of the shops were sporting French flags. It was all very strange, and she continued on doggedly until she found a chemist's shop. She tripped as she came out of the shop, and cursed as she hurt her ribs and aching arm. She looked around with a worried frown, had she sworn in French or English? Nobody was watching her, they were all hurrying about their own business, in actual fact it all seemed very busy, and one presumably old person staggering around did not raise any interest. The assistant in the shop had been very helpful, and she was soon making her way out of town, to find the rest of her belongings which were hidden in a hedgerow. She popped a couple of painkillers into her mouth, and drank from her bottle. Now she could move on, and try to heal her aching body. She couldn't wait to use the bandages she had just bought around her aching chest, as they should be more comfortable than the strips of cotton underskirt.

CHAPTER SEVENTEEN

30th April 1945 was one of the Reich's final days, the Allies arrived in Berlin and this was followed by news that the Fuehrer ('that bloodthirsty guttersnipe' as Churchill had called him) had killed himself. The Red Flag flew over the Richstag building in Berlin on V-Day. In London on 13th May nothing had been said officially but Britain took to the streets to celebrate victory. All at once the privation and misery of five wartime years were forgotten in a colourful blaze of flags, fireworks and floodlights – the end of hostilities in Europe. Earlier in the month General Montgomery and Bedell Smith had accepted Germany's final surrender.

An election was planned for the 5th July, the first general election since 1935 when the coalition government ruled.

Evan John spent some time at home, and then returned to the RAF where there was still much to be done. However, Jerome now had only one priority, and that was to find his wife Sarah Kate. Now that the War had ended, knowing that it would be months and years before things got back to a reasonably normal state, he was nevertheless determined to

157

get things moving. He had been asked to stay on with the RAF at least for a few months, but he was not having any. He camped outside the *big house*, determined that he would eventually get a meeting with Sarah Kate's Commanding Officer.

One strange occurrence which gave Jerome and Evan some hope was the fact that Zeke Williams had returned from the War, but he had then gone back to France where he and his men had been helped by a French farming family. On leaving the area after being warned by the family that the Germans were only minutes away, Zeke had turned back to see a pall of smoke over the farmhouse, and he had worried ever since what had happened to that family who had helped his men get away from the area when vastly outnumbered, to enable them to fight another day.

On his return to find that family and farmhouse, he had found that the mother and daughter were still well, and trying to carry on working the farm. They informed him that when the Germans had arrived during the War hot on the heels of Zeke and his men, that following a bout of brutality and antagonism from the Germans, the farmer had succumbed to a heart attack and died, and because of that the Germans had suddenly moved on, leaving the mother and daughter to cope with the death of their loved one, and a burning farm!

Zeke stayed with the family for a few weeks to help them work extensively on the farmhouse, and the farm buildings – mainly the barn, and he managed to get them back into working order, so that they might live more comfortably. During that time he had accompanied Julienne the daughter of the family to try to get supplies both for the building work and food. They entered a village, by the name of Sainte Pierre when it was a market day. Whilst there waiting for Julienne to make her purchases, he heard a voice curse in

English. He had been amazed, and had then tried to find that person, but to no avail. He had also returned the following market day but without any success, and he never heard any further words spoken in English. Upon reflection Zeke thought that that voice had a northern accent, and he mentioned this strange occurrence to Evan John and Jerome on his return to England. Everyone in the valley was aware that no word had been received from Sarah Kate Evans for many years, and Zeke hoped that this information might in some way be useful to Evan John and Jerome in their quest to find Sarah Kate, it was a long shot, but hell these were very strange times.

All this was remarkable because Zeke had returned home after the War to be told by Megs that whilst he was away, there had been a tragedy at home, and his mother-in-law, and his wife had perished in a snow storm whilst they tried to travel home from Grasmere. His children had survived because of the hard work and determination of Evan Evans and the men of the valley who had searched for them. The two children had been put between the grown ups, and wrapped in their mother's coat and had survived, and they had improved in health due to the care and attention they had received from Zeke's relatives and Sarah and Megs Evans. Zeke Williams had found it very difficult to get to know his daughter Elizabeth, who was very like her mother, but she had been born whilst he was away fighting, and her existence was a complete surprise to him. It didn't help that young Elizabeth was very close with Megs – Megs the girl that Zeke had been very attracted to, but before he had properly realised this, his previous behaviour during the early years of the War had made this impossible.

Jerome Graham, who had volunteered to fly with the RAF shortly after the start of the War, was Canadian and his second language was French. He was, therefore, determined to leave the RAF and go in search of his wife. All he needed was some sort of idea where she might be from the men who had trained her, and who it seemed to him, had *forgotten* her!

For over a week Jerome had camped outside the *big house*, and had become quite friendly with the red caps on duty there, however, they would not let him in to the building. On the eighth day, Jerome was a little confused, he was coughing and had a high temperature - he was obviously suffering from some sort of illness, which made him slightly delirious. The red caps were becoming aware that he was really ill, and one of them went inside to report to their superiors.

After some considerable time a distinguished looking RAF Wing Commander came outside to see the Canadian Squadron Leader. He placed his hand on the younger man's forehead, and grimaced he was obviously running a high temperature.

"Get an RAF ambulance here as soon as possible," the Wing Commander ordered the red cap. "In the meantime you had better bring him into my office."

The Wing Commander watched as Jerome was helped inside, and bent down to pick up a photograph he saw on the cold step of the building where Jerome had been sleeping, obviously dropped by the Canadian. He stared at it for a couple of minutes then drew in a deep breath, what was he to do? He looked at the wedding photograph of Sarah Kate Evans, now Graham. When the War was in progress he had no doubts about his decisions being correct. However, in the cold light of day with the hostilities over, he did have doubts. Slowly he moved towards the doorway, and turned to find a worried Evan John Evans with a look of determination on his face. Yes, this young man and the one indoors had fought hard and long for Britain and the Allies. Dozens of their RAF colleagues, both pilots and crew had perished over the last five years. These two had been lucky, only in the sense that they had survived, both had been shot down and suffered the scars, and in the Wing Commander's opinion they needed a little bit more luck.

He indicated that Evan John should accompany him inside the building.

The RAF ambulance arrived, and after about an hour, when they had done what they could for the young Squadron Leader, they left again, as he had flatly refused to go into hospital. Jerome was now feeling slightly better after taking a number of painkillers for his head, and normally he would have felt like falling into a nice warm bed. However, Jerome hoped that his long vigil outside these premises had now worked, as the Wing Commander returned to join himself and Evan John, and sat down opposite them, and was obviously having trouble deciding how to begin this conversation.

Jerome couldn't wait any longer. "I am looking for my wife, who I know has been working for you as a Code and Cipher Officer, but we think it is much more than that. My colleague here, as I think you probably know, is Evan John Evans her twin brother." Jerome, looked up at Evan John as he joined his brother-in law, and put his hand on his shoulder. Jerome continued, encouraged by the fact that the Wing Commander had not stopped him from talking.

"My wife and I had only been married for three months, when I was presumed dead, but I had survived the burning plane, and then the crash. When I regained consciousness, and told them at the hospital a few days later my name, I was shattered to find that my wife had been informed of my death, and she had left this town and probably this country." Again the Wing Commander had nothing to say, however, he did look particularly uncomfortable – something was bothering him. He was silent for a short while, and then

161

stabbed his pen into the pad in front of him, and lifted his eyes.

"What I am about to tell you is completely confidential. I am aware that you have both signed the necessary forms regarding secrecy and I remind you now that secrecy is still of paramount importance." The Wing Commander paused. It might be the end of his career, but he meant to help these young men, and if at all possible Sarah Kate, whose confident gaze had hurt him deeply as she walked away towards the Lysander aircraft. She had obviously been grieving for her husband, and he had let her go because he *had* to, she might be a small part of a large whole, but what she was being sent away for was important to the whole country and the hopeful end of the War. He had *deliberately* not told her that her husband had survived the crash! Hopefully he could do something to make him feel better, and these too young men!

"We have not heard from your wife at all in the last few months, at this time we do not know where she is. We have not been able to contact the person who might know her whereabouts. That is about all I can *tell* you at the moment." He hoped that his tone intimated that he wanted to help, and if they could read between the lines maybe he could! He was confident that they were very intelligent young men and both on a mission to find Sarah Kate Graham.

"We have been told by an officer with the Border Regiment, that recently whilst in France after the War, he heard a smattering of English spoken, which of course drew his attention, as he recognised the accent as someone from the North of England." Jerome said feeling slightly more hopeful that this man could help, it didn't seem as though he was going to have them thrown out again.

"There is really nothing more I can tell you. We are in touch with someone over there who is trying to make contact with people in another area, near where our contact was. I can't say anything, but what area in France did your soldier friend visit?"

"He was in the area around Sainte Pierre, a small village, not far from Verneuil to the North West of Paris. Do you suppose that would be a good place to start a search?" Jerome asked, as it seemed clear that the Wing Commander wanted to help, but he too had been sworn to secrecy. Compared to the British Isles, France was a very large country, but compared to Canada maybe it wasn't so big!

The Wing Commander sat doodling on the blotter before him, and then he put down the pen and put his head in his hands. Suddenly he sat up straight and murmured 'excuse me' and left the room. His tone intimated that he was coming back.

Evan and Jerome looked at each other with raised brows. Wondering whether or not they were going to receive any help or information, but both realising the difficult position the other man was in!

"Do you feel better Jerome, we can't do anything until you are well again, and I get some time off. I shouldn't have said I might be signing on again." Evan wanted to be with Jerome if he really was going to France. He desperately wanted to find his twin, but he also wanted to be there for Jerome if the news was not so good!

"I feel a lot better Evan, I think we may be getting somewhere, he didn't say 'yes' or 'no' to Sainte Pierre, I think he knows something but can't tell us outright. It's hard to take Evan, we have both flown over France scores and scores of times, now when we need to go it will be long slog by other means."

"I really meant are you physically feeling better, I guess that you are!"

The Wing Commander came back into the office, still with an enigmatic expression in his eyes. Then briefly he smiled.

"Well, I guess you know that a number of men managed to get back home after escaping from Prisoner of War camps over the last two or three years, when the Germans had over-run Europe? When they arrived back they were de-briefed, and whatever they had to say was noted and filed away for future reference. I can tell you that *some* of those accounts were quite illuminating. The route they took to get back to this country and the people they met on the way were of specific interest to us." He continued after a moment, again doodling on his blotter, with something on his mind.

"You had a question you wanted to ask me, before I left the room?" The Wing Commander said blandly with raised eyes.

"Is Sainte Pierre, a village near to Verneuil, an interesting place?" Evan said quickly, whilst Jerome stared at the Wing Commander.

"I couldn't possibly say Flying Officer Evans. I suggest you see your Wing Commander he may have something of interest to say to you." The Wing Commander stood, and extended his hand to shake that of Evan John, and then turned to Jerome who had managed to stand. He shook Jerome's hand, and turned the blotter the other way around on his desk.

"Good luck gentlemen," the older man said, with an enigmatic smile as he left the room. He caught sight of himself reflected in the glass window in the door, goodness me, he was turning quite grey, and no wonder.

Jerome quickly studied the blotter, and then pulled out the top sheet, with a big grin at his brother-in-law. "Let's go and see why you should see your Commanding Officer Evan."

"Let's have a look at the blotter Jerome, I hope it isn't too smudged, from the look on your face it is good news." Evan said, as he helped Jerome outside, where the two red caps saluted them!

"I don't know exactly, there are one or two names, which mean nothing at the moment. However, Sainte Pierre is ringed, and the rest is a lot of doodling, but we will have to peruse it finely to make sure that's all it is," he really smiled, it was a smile of anticipation, and Evan John hoped he would not be disappointed.

Evan John helped Jerome into his car, and then walked around to get in the other side. He too felt a lift of spirits, there was a chance that they might find Sarah Kate, but he had a niggling doubt, as he wondered why she had not managed to get home now that the War had ended? Although he was unaware of where she had been or what she was doing on her first trip she had managed to get back unharmed. He realised that the ferocity of the war had escalated, and it had only been realised how dreadful it had been when the Nazi Death Camps had been discovered. He was aware that now many German civilians were being taken to view the death camps by force, as they would *not accept* what had happened. A mass extermination which many refused to admit ever took place, was shown to them when they were forced to view the gas chambers which SS Guards called bathhouses, and ovens in which thousands of victims were cremated. Evan pulled his thoughts together, he should not dwell on these atrocities which had shocked the world – Sarah *would* be found and soon!

Jerome drew his car up outside his lodgings, and Mrs Brown was there at the door waiting for them.

She had been wonderfully kind and understanding since he had returned 'from the dead.' Mrs Brown was anxious that both these young men should find out the truth, and then they could get on with their lives. The lives that they had risked nearly every day for the last four or five years!

Jerome felt well enough to have a bath, and change of clothes. He was anxious to see Evan's Wing Commander. Mrs Brown insisted that they both had something to eat before she would let them out of 13 Lime Street, which they really appreciated later. She also extracted promises that they would keep in touch with her.

CHAPTER EIGHTEEN

Sarah Kate staggered the last few yards to the riverbank, the water was rippling over the rounded stones, and it was like music to her ears. Cool, cool water and she could fill her bottle, and refresh her body. She had been so hot, so hot she couldn't bear it. She knelt beside the river, and held the bottle under the water, and watched as the bubbles came to the surface, and she wondered if she could catch them they were so pretty. It took her a couple of minutes to get the cork in the bottle, but she knew it was important, she had forgotten why, but it was important. She placed it safely on the bank of the river.

She dipped her face in the water, it was good, but she must not get wet all over as she wanted, as Great Grandma Kate would not approve. She closed her eyes, and tried to think – was Great Grandma Kate dead now, she couldn't remember? Her mother wouldn't mind her getting wet, and she would soon dry, and it was so very hot. She lowered herself into the river, and revelled in the coolness, and how clean her body felt.

She thought she could hear a horse and cart on the track, she must keep quiet, she mustn't be discovered or the Marsaud family and Marianne and Jacques, and maybe the missing Jean Distelle would be in danger. Maybe she *should* let herself go, and float away on the cool water, she could float to join Jerome, he would welcome her with open arms, he was waiting for her, and she really *needed* him, it would be so easy.

She suddenly pulled herself towards the bank of the river. She might be able to climb out of this river which was getting colder and colder, and she *should* because Evan John and her Dad would not approve of her being such a wimp, they were so proud of her, and she couldn't let Megs down.

The sound of horse hooves in the distance reminded her where she was, and she pulled herself up onto the bank, and let the water run from her body. It was a few minutes before she could get together the strength to push back her hair and run her fingers through it. Her chest and ribs should feel better when the bandage started to dry, it would tighten up. She got to her feet groggily, and noticed some berries on a bush. She picked them and put them straight into her mouth. They were good, and she had a little piece of bread left which she would eat even if she had to wet it with water from her trusty bottle, just so long as she could get back across the cart track, and find her things.

She put her hand to her thigh - yes her knife was still there. She wasn't sure if she loved it or hated it. She dreamt about it and what it had done, but it hadn't done that horrible thing alone. She sighed and strived to block out the graphic images that were in her mind of Heinrich Schiller and Wilhelm Schmidt. She would concentrate and think of Evan John and try to get him to come here for her, he would be so relieved to find her because she hadn't been able to get in touch with him, and he must wonder why. No, that was not the right thing to do, because if she did that she would be putting him in danger, and Mam, Dad and Megs would never forgive her. When she had eaten her bread, she would drink from her bottle, and think of Jerome, who was patiently waiting for her to come and join him eventually.

She managed to get to her feet, and looked left and right, and when nothing was coming along the track, she tried to hurry across towards the barn, with her precious bottle of water held limply in her hand. She almost felt safe when she reached the barn door, but was very worried that she wouldn't have the strength to climb up into the hay.

CHAPTER NINETEEN

Jerome had bathed and dressed in clean civilian clothes, and he and Evan had eaten making them feel much better. He and Evan John had been waiting outside the office of Evan's Commanding Officer, and his own ex-Commanding Officer for over an hour. Both men had felt really excited and looking forward to something exciting turning up, but with this long wait they were now starting to suffer from anxiety. They were both asked to enter the office, and looked at each other in surprise and then did as they were bid. They were then asked to take a seat, which they did.

An hour later everything had been resolved, at least for the time being.

Evan John had been given three weeks rest and recuperation, this time to be filled with the search for his twin sister.

Jerome Graham had been 'recruited' by the RAF which he had only just left, for a further six months, and his first task was to find his wife, together with the help of his brother-in-law, and he would have to change into uniform once more. Not only that, they were to be taken to France in a Lysander aircraft which would land on the nearest aerodrome to Verneuil, and they had received the impression that this was alright, as that was how Sarah Kate was supposed to have been returned to this country a very long time ago!

The next morning at first light, they were being ushered onto the small aircraft, both wearing uniform. Strangely they were both nervous, being used to piloting their own planes, and the man travelling with them told them he was normally the dispatcher, the man who made sure the parachutists left the plane safely. He pointed out the intercom which the pilot used to contact him, showed them the hole in the floor of the fuselage where the person parachuting sat with legs dangling, and the hook on which the static line of the jumper's parachute was hitched, and the red light which turned to green before the agent would drop from the plane, at about 400 to 300 feet!

The ex dispatcher looked at the two pilots. "Did you ever have to parachute to safety?"

"My brother in law here managed to ditch his Spitfire in the sea, and was rescued by a fishing boat. I went down with mine, it was on fire, it hit a tall tree and I was thrown out, luckily before the whole thing exploded." Jerome looked at Evan John, "Did you every consider parachuting?"

"No, I never gave it a thought, as I hoped I might find a way to save the plane! By the way I never thought about it before, but either 300 or 400 feet is hardly high enough to parachute from. Still I guess they had to go in low or be detected."

Much later two very thoughtful young men *walked* away from the plane with grateful thanks to the pilot and dispatcher, having landed on the nearest aerodrome to the town of Verneuil, nothing had been said but it was more than likely that Sarah Kate had arrived in France in a Lysander!

They were now on their own, and walked into Verneuil. They found a garage, and were offered a vehicle that had been left by the Germans. Fuel was hard to come by, but when they left the garage, they had a reliable vehicle and a full tank of fuel, and a happy garage man whose family would eat well tonight, awaiting their return in a couple of weeks.

Evan had only taken French at grammar school, so Jerome who had lived beside that language for most of his life took over the enquiries. They were hailed as heroes in Verneuil in their RAF uniforms, but when they started enquiring about Jean Distelle, and where could he be found, they hit a brick wall. They were disappointed, as now that the War was over, surely anyone who had worked with the Resistance would be a valued citizen. An old lady in black, with a tanned and lined face, heard them asking about Jean Distelle, and she indicated that they should visit with the Mayor of Verneuil, who would decide if they were to be made welcome or not! According to the old lady the Mayor had been useless during the years since the Germans had walked through their country before and after the Armistice with Hitler. The Mayor should now start earning his crust!

They found the town hall, and after being introduced to the Mayor (a rather pompous and self important man) they enquired where they might find Jean Distelle.

"Gentlemen, it had been brought to my notice that Monsieur Jean Distelle has not been seen for nearly two months now. A young woman Mademoiselle Marianne Flamand has been asking the police if they know where he is. Unfortunately, they do not know anything and Mademoiselle Flamand is very worried, he was supposed to call on her, and also Monsieur Distelle's mother is anxious as she has not seen her son, for many months. Unfortunately, Monsieur Distelle Jean's father, was killed by

172

the German secret police, during the War. The German's have gone and still we are in turmoil," the Mayor said and watched as Jerome made a note of the name Marianne Flamand.

Jerome and Evan then went through the list they had taken off the blotter, and realised that her name was not included. Jerome made a big ring around it.

"Where may we find Mademoiselle Flamand?" Jerome asked hopefully.

"She is sometimes in Verneuil as this is the nearest town, but she lives in a village a few miles way, Sainte Pierre."

Evan and Jerome looked at each other, and tried not to look too hopeful.

During their interview with the Mayor, Jerome produced a wedding photograph, and explained that his wife in the photograph was the person they were seeking. The Mayor glanced at it briefly, and then he took it to the window and looked at it more closely. He looked shocked, and then angry, and stamped out of the room, and only returned after shouting loudly at one of his minions. He returned to his office where Evan and Jerome looked at him enquiringly. Something must have set him off, he was angry, but not with them it seemed!

"I would be obliged if you would wait here gentlemen. I may be able to help you later. I have ordered some refreshments to be brought to you." He left the room, after perusing the photograph once again, shaking his head and muttering to himself.

Both Evan and Jerome were anxious to go to Sainte Pierre and try to find Marianne Flamand. She had been looking for Jean Distelle, so in the absence of this gentleman she was the only clue they had!

There was a bit of a commotion outside the Mayor's Office, and then the door was opened and in walked a man about fifty years old looking flustered and annoyed, followed by the Mayor with a very stern expression on his florid face.

"I have baking to finish, Mayor, what can be so urgent that you have sent for me in this manner," Gerrard Marsaud said angrily. The Mayor had kept a low profile during the years of German occupation, now he was here throwing his weight about! The Mayor took Gerrard by the arm, turning him and indicating that there were two other people there.

"This is Gerrard Marsaud, the local baker. These gentlemen have come to France looking for this man's wife and this man's sister," the Mayor said pointing at the young men, and then handing the wedding photograph to Gerrard.

"Violette Marsaud, where is she? She was sometimes sad and I got the impression she was a widow," Gerrard said both surprised and visibly upset.

"You say her name is Violette Marsaud? Don't you know where she is?" Jerome and Evan almost spoke as one.

"She had to leave us, after the trouble at the Chateau. A Gestapo Officer died suddenly, and there was a possibility that she might have been blamed. I don't know where she is perhaps Jean Distelle will know." Gerrard was becoming very worried, he remembered that Violette had told them, but he must not tell her husband and her brother. What had happened during the War was in a totally different environment. If she ever wanted them to know, if she could be found, then she could tell them herself. He must change the subject. "She took the place of my cousin, and lived at the bakery with myself and my mother." Gerrard paused briefly.

"I can tell you are her brother, you have the same eyes. I believed that she was a widow, although she never said much about herself." Gerrard looked at Jerome and Evan worriedly.

174

"As you can see from our uniforms we are both RAF pilots. Unfortunately, my wife was told that I was dead, because that is what they all believed. My plane went down in a ball of flames, luckily I survived. However, my wife was sent to France before I had regained consciousness in hospital, she never knew that I had survived."

"Poor Violette, she is a wonderful person. You are looking for Violette Marsaud whilst you are in France. She assumed my young cousin's identity. My cousin was violated by the Germans, and very soon after she hung herself. The fact that she killed herself was not widely known, as her mother was determined that her papers were used, in order to get back at the Germans. That is what I must now explain to the Mayor, and why he seems so angry," Gerrard said with an apologetic look towards the Mayor. "If you should find Violette please can you let us know, as myself and my mother, known to her as Aunt Bridgette, have been hoping to hear from her, but she wouldn't want to put us in danger," Gerrard finished with a hopeless sigh. It was weeks since the War had ended, and she should have been in touch!

"I don't understand why she hasn't been in touch with someone, now that the War is over." Evan John said. "It should have been safe for her to return to you Monsieur Marsaud after the Germans had left?"

"Jean Distelle is missing. He kept in touch with me, Violette, and Jacques and Marianne Flamand. Without Jean your only hope of ever finding Violette is if Marianne and Jacques know anything. I wish you luck." Gerrard said and it was plain that he was very upset, as he stood to shake hands with both Evan and Jerome, and then after a brief look to gauge the situation, the Mayor.

The Mayor shook hands with Evan and Jerome and extracted a promise that they would keep in touch. The

Mayor shouted for someone to come into the office, and they provided Jerome and Evan with a map of the area, and then helpfully pointed out Sainte Pierre, in relation to Verneuil.

The Mayor provided them with his calling card, and insisted that they should get in touch whatever they found in Sainte Pierre. They had wondered if they should find somewhere to stay overnight, as it was late afternoon, but decided they could always sleep in the vehicle if necessary. They couldn't wait to get to Sainte Pierre, and find Mademoiselle Marianne Flamand, and hopefully, Violette Marsaud!

They parked their vehicle on a narrow street and walked down the street until they came to the market square. Locals were putting up stalls, presumably ready for the morning, which must be market day.

Evan and Jerome walked around the square, asking if anyone had seen Violette Marsaud. The people tried to be helpful, but if they had known her, she had not been seen for a while. It was becoming dusk when Jerome suddenly realised that they should be asking for Marianne Flamand, not Violette. This request was received with success, and they were directed to a cottage at the end of the village.

Evan looked around the small village, and noticed all the French flags which were in evidence. Now the War was ended there seemed to be a new endeavour to get back their nationality and celebrate it. Evan wondered what it must have been like to live through German occupation for so many years. He also wondered what Sarah Kate had suffered. He was still mulling over the information which Gerrard Marsaud had given regarding the Chateau, and how obvious it had been that he wished he had kept his mouth shut. Gerrard was loyal to Violette, and he wondered what Marianne and Jacques would be like, if they were as loyal then it might be difficult to find anything out about Violette.

When the door opened he was not prepared for either of them!

Jacques opened the door, and Evan was surprised by the thin, ill looking man, who was grey at the temples, and Evan assumed that he was much older than he was. As for Marianne who stood behind her brother, he was knocked out. Her beautiful eyes held him mesmerised as they stared into his.

"Hello," Jerome said in a friendly fashion. "Sorry to disturb you, but we are looking for Marianne and Jacques Flamand."

They both looked wary, and then Jacques nodded slowly. Evan and Marianne were both having trouble looking away from each other. She was mesmerised by his eyes, she thought she had seen them somewhere before. Evan thought she was the most beautiful young woman he had seen in a very long time.

"I am Jacques Flamand, and this is my sister Marianne," Jacques said, and after a couple of seconds he opened the door so that they might step inside.

The cottage was quite small, but homely, and Evan could tell that Marianne was worried as she looked at their uniforms.

"As you can see I am English, and my friend Jerome is Canadian. We have both been fighting the Germans, and we are with the RAF Fighter Command." Evan said, and he felt the atmosphere in the cottage lighten considerably. "I am looking for my sister and wonder if you can help."

He was a bit nonplussed as Marianne kept staring at him, and he looked back and after a few seconds, he saw recognition dawn in her lovely eyes.

"Violette," Marianne said wonderingly. "I knew I had seen your eyes before. Won't you please both sit down?"

They all sat around the table, and Marianne continued to look worried, as she stared into Evan's eyes, almost but not quite the eyes that she had seen many times before, many times showing the same expression of deep concern, and always for someone else.

Evan could see from Marianne's eyes that all was not well, and he wondered what Jerome would do if Marianne and her brother were unable to help them in their search, they seemed to be running out of names and options! Her next words made him feel even more worried.

"We have not seen Violette for many weeks. We have been trying to contact the leader of the Resistance in this area, for the last ten days. He seems to have disappeared, and so has Violette."

This was much worse that Evan John had been expecting, and his glance at Jerome was a very worried one. They must try to keep things together, or they would never find Sarah Kate, or ever know what had happened to her. They must persevere or it would be impossible for them to go back home! He reached out to Jerome, as he turned his devastated gaze towards him. They could not, and would not give up now, as Sarah Kate (Violette) must need them.

CHAPTER TWENTY

Jerome put his elbows on the table and held his head in his hands. He looked thoroughly dejected, and as he lifted his head a muscle flicked in the side of his autocratic jaw, he looked as if this was the last straw.

"My friend has been unwell, do you think we might have a drink, we have had nothing except a drink and small cake in the Mayor's Office in Verneuil, since we arrived in France." Evan said with a glance at Jacques, who also looked unwell, and then his eyes were drawn to Marianne. Marianne jumped up from the table and went into a room at the back of the cottage. They could hear her running water, and then the sound of crockery being prepared.

"You are welcome to share what we have, which I'm afraid is not a lot," Jacques said with a wry smile. "Are you going to introduce your friend and yourself?"

"Of course, I am Evan John Evans, the twin of Sarah Kate and 'Violette.' This is Jerome Graham, and he is Canadian and volunteered to fly with the RAF in the early stages of the War. He is my brother-in-law, and therefore, Sarah Kate and 'Violette's' husband." Evan looked up to see

Marianne's shocked face in the doorway. It became very obvious that Sarah Kate had only told these good people the bare necessities, both for her own and for their safety.

"Can you explain things Jerome, whilst I go to the car and bring back the provisions we picked up in Verneuil?" Evan asked as he slowly left the small cottage.

When he had picked up the bags of provisions and returned to the small cottage, Evan realised that Jerome had told them about his 'death' and the fact that Sarah Kate had already left the country when he had regained consciousness, and therefore, Sarah Kate (Violette) was not aware that her husband had *survived* the plane crash. Marianne was crying quietly, and Evan felt a great need to take her in his arms to comfort her. What had gotten into him, he had to stay calm and sensible both for himself, Jerome and Sarah Kate if she was to be found.

Marianne looked at the shopping bags in awe, it was obvious that provisions were still in very short supply in France, or maybe it was the money to pay for them. He handed a bag to her, and she pulled out cheese and some sort of sausage, bread and fruit, and then moved back into the room at the back of the house. Evan was pleased they had thought to equip themselves for any emergency, money in your pocket was still a necessity - they had thought they might need to bribe someone for information.

Marianne brought the food to the table, with a large pot of coffee and the two pilots enjoyed their first French meal. Afterwards, the crockery and remaining food was cleared away by Marianne and Jacques, and they returned to the table. They had obviously been talking together in the back room, or kitchen area.

"We have decided that now the War is over, it will be alright to tell you everything we know about 'Violette,' sorry but to us she is Violette. When she jumped from the aircraft we were there to meet her, and help her to bury her parachute and to carry away the wireless sets, and incendiary devices she had brought with her, and she became our sister, Violette Flamand." Jacques said, and looked at the almost shocked expressions on the faces of the young men listening avidly.

"I don't think we ever realised how dangerous and difficult it would be living in an *occupied* country. I guess we were fighting to avoid that, and to help those already occupied by the Germans. Sorry, please carry on." Jerome looked a bit bewildered as if he couldn't place his lovely wife with the intrepid, and when he listened further, indomitable woman Jacques was talking about!

"Violette kept in contact with London on the wireless set, and sent and received coded messages. With her incendiary devices we managed to blow up an ammunition dump belonging to the Germans, and then to de-rail an ammunitions train, and then things were getting more difficult in this area, and she became Violette Marsaud with that girl's authentic papers and she travelled to the coast and then in a fishing boat back to England. She told us this when she returned to France, again as Violette Marsaud. This time she stayed with her 'cousin' Gerrard Marsaud and his mother. Things happened and it became dangerous for her in Verneuil, and Jean Distelle arranged for her to visit Violette's real mother, to help with the transportation of prisoners of war trying to get to England via 'safe houses.' That was the last time Marianne saw her, as she was still keeping a low profile, as were we." Jacques finished, and looked at the mesmerised faces of his visitors. Jacques had spoken slowly and Evan John had managed to understand most of it, with only a little help from Jerome.

"Can we visit this Madame Marsaud, it must have been very difficult for her to have Violette to stay with her, as it would be a reminder of the death of her *real* daughter every day." Evan said shaking his head.

"We can visit with Madame Marsaud, but not tonight, she is old and will not appreciate being disturbed, even though the Germans have all left this area. We had the Gestapo, the German Secret Police, in this area and they have searched the Marsaud Farm often. You can sleep here until morning." Marianne said, and looked at the small sofa and chairs.

"Thank you Marianne, I will sleep in the back of the car, and Evan can stretch out on the sofa with the help of a chair." Jerome said looking slightly mesmerised by all he had heard, he wanted to be alone and think about everything that had been said.

Evan John and Jerome both had a disturbed nights sleep. In the morning after a meal of croissants and fruit brought from the village shop, all four climbed into the car, and Jerome drove them with Marianne giving directions. When they reached the bridge before the turn-off to the farm she asked Jerome to stop the car. She climbed out and the others followed her. None of the group of four heard the pleasant sound of birdsong, or the whisper of water over stones, or feel the warm sun on their faces, their only thoughts were of Sarah Kate.

"There was an accident here, a Gestapo armoured car driven by two men from Chateau Genevieve near Verneuil were injured. The bicycle from the farm Marsaud was smashed and found on the road, but there was no blood on the road. The two men were taken away by the Gestapo as they had been hurt, but not fatally, and the car was towed away as it had ended up in the river. Violette seems to have vanished since that time, and that is why I have been so anxious to find Jean Distelle in case he knows something!" Marianne finished speaking, and paused. "I'm sorry, but maybe we should continue by seeing Madame Marsaud, she might have something to add."

They went back to the car without anyone saying a word, and it was a morose party that arrived at the farm Marsaud five minutes later.

Marianne knocked at the door, and when Madame opened it she introduced the men with her, and Madame promptly burst into tears, and chattered so fast that even Jerome had trouble following her outburst. She led the way around to the pigsty, and lifted a wooden door and indicated inside.

"Madame Marsaud says that she believes that someone hid here after the accident, she thinks it may have been Violette as no prisoners-of-war have passed through since the War ended." Marianne said with a slight smile wondering where Violette could have hidden herself away since she slept in the pigsty. Both Evan John and Jerome looked shocked as they visualised what Sarah Kate had gone through, and very much alone it seemed at the moment.

They all thanked Madame Marsaud, and promised they would let her know if they found Violette, and then they drove back in the car to the bridge, and Jerome stopped for another look around. Marianne showed them underneath the bridge where some of the prisoners-of-war had hidden, but there was nothing on the walls or anywhere around that Violette might have left, or written.

"She can't just disappear," Evan John said in desperation. God he needed to know where she was, his feelings were in tumult, as one minute he thought she was near, the next he believed he might never find her alive. Why wasn't their unique twin connection working, had she been killed by the car driven by the Gestapo?

"It seems she was trained to do a lot of things we know nothing about," Jerome said beginning to wonder if he would

183

know this woman if they found her! His heart was breaking, and he had a dreadful feeling that whatever they did, or found, it would be too late. "Where did she stay in France, except for Madame Marsaud's farm?"

"She stayed one night with us, and the rest of the time at the cafe and bakery Marsaud in Veneuil." Marianne said near to tears, it tore at her heart to see these strong men so distressed, but staunchly determined to carry on with their quest.

The three men rested against the wall of the bridge, and Marianne sat down by the water's edge, her mind in turmoil, she must be able to help these young men.

Jacques suddenly stood up and gazed at Marianne hopefully.

"The barn, Marianne the barn, where she stayed the very first night, and from where she sent wireless messages to London, on her first visit to France," Jacques said excitedly, "it's the only place left to look."

"But by the look of the bicycle that was found on the road, she might have been terribly injured, how would she get so far?" Marianne said hopelessly.

"Is it far?" Jerome asked trying not to be too hopeful, as his heart started once again on its more usual rhythm.

"The other side of Sainte Pierre, we should be near there in thirty minutes, we might not be able to get the car very near." Jacques said and they all piled into the car, and Jerome turned it around in a gateway, and they drove off. The journey was only for about twenty five minutes, but it seemed like forever to Jerome as he negotiated the narrow cart track.

They left the car and approached the barn. Marianne was dreading what they might find, it was weeks since Violette had been seen, and quite possible she *had* been badly hurt by the accident with the Gestapo armoured car. Still Marianne

184

was determined to get into the barn and up onto the highest level before either the brother or the husband. There was no knowing what they might find, but most likely nothing!

They moved towards the barn door, and Marianne had never felt so wound up and excited since she had been in the thick of their Resistance work. She noticed with a deep disappointment that there was no carefully placed piece of straw near the door opening, which she remembered seeing Violette place carefully where it would be disturbed if anyone tried to open the door. It seemed that Violette was not here.

Jacques opened the barn door, and moved across to the ladder, and when Evan and Jerome both tried to use it he stopped them, and indicated that Marianne should climb the ladder, only Marianne for the time being.

Marianne moved forward slowly her heart in her mouth, and then she heard a dry cough, a slight rustling sound, and a murmur. She moved quickly forward and stopped dead in her tracks. Violette was crouched low, and in her hand she held a small knife, which she was moving dangerously from side to side. "Get away from me Wilhelm Schmidt," she hissed in French. Her eyes were slightly glazed and Marianne realised she was very sick.

"Violette, it's me Marianne, and Jacques, don't worry everything is alright, the German's have gone, the War is over," Marianne promised, and heard the others close behind her.

"Go away Marianne, and take Jacques, it's not safe," Sarah Kate said tiredly, she coughed and held her side, lowering the knife. Marianne took the knife from her, and Evan moved forward with his heart in his mouth, his twin was in a bad way, but she was alive!

"Sarah Kate, I have come to take you home, it's me Evan John."

"No Evan's not here, I would know, give me the password," Sarah Kate said, and they realised she was delirious and possibly slipping in and out of consciousness, and strangely Evan John felt a kind of relief, semi-consciousness must be the reason she couldn't sense *he* was near, and equally why he had not been able to connect with her! He had never thought that she was dead, but had not dared to say anything in case this connection between himself and his twin had disappeared.

"Can you remember Violette's password Jacques?" Marianne asked quickly, desperately wanting to help her friend.

"Something I didn't understand, something about peas."

Evan moved forward, and took his sister's hand. "Was it *shelling peas* Sarah Kate, like Great Grandma Kate used to say about Aunt Marjorie giving birth? It *is me* Evan John, you can feel it now." He stated, as her contorted and distressed face slowly relaxed.

Sarah lay back in exhaustion, and relaxed, with tears running down her pale cheeks. "I'll go home with *you* Evan, I was going to join Jerome but maybe it *is* too soon." She sighed deeply, and seemed to fall asleep, and her breathing was quite regular Evan noticed with relief.

Evan had tears running down his cheeks, and he glanced at Jerome who was standing at the top of the ladder, not daring to appear until his wife had been told that her husband was alive, and he was wracked by emotion, as his wife had been contemplating joining him in death!

Marianne looked at her own brother who looked absolutely devastated - it seemed it was up to her and 'Violette,' or Sarah Kate as her brother had called her. Sarah Kate was obviously ill, and they needed to care for her.

Jerome was looking absolutely poleaxed, he couldn't understand what was going on, there was his Sarah Kate and he needed to touch her, to reassure himself that she was really his wife and show her that he loved her, and *they* were talking about 'shelling peas.' He desperately wanted to show her how much he loved and needed her, but so much had been happening in her life which might have changed her and how she felt, as she had believed herself to be a widow, and she still did, and besides that his body was scarred!

Marianne looked around her in dismay, nobody seemed to know how to proceed with this traumatic situation, she had always believed it was the female species that were the most emotional, but she seemed to have been misinformed. "Jacques you go and fetch a doctor as quickly as possible for Violette, Evan must stay here with his twin, and so Jerome will have to drive you. You must bring something for Violette to eat and drink, she will have had very little to eat for days. And you Evan John had better think of what to tell your sister when she wakens out of her sudden and healing sleep. If the doctor says I can look after her with her husband's help, then you and Jacques had better stay at the Farm with Madame Marsaud for a few days." She watched as Jacques and a very reluctant Jerome, moved down the ladder. Jerome *had* to drive, and was aware that Sarah Kate, particularly in her apparently fragile state, would have to be prepared before she met him, and he obviously was not going to wait very long!

Evan stared at the lovely girl, who had helped them so much. Yes, he would try to decide how to tell his sister that her husband was alive, and well, and still loving her to distraction, without causing her too much distress – it would not be easy. He watched her as she slept, and after about ten minutes, she stirred and stared at his face almost in disbelief, then she closed her eyes again, as Evan John glanced at

187

Marianne, and she smiled back at him, confirming to him that she thought Sarah Kate was safe and only sleeping.

"Marianne, thank you for everything, I must explain things to Sarah Kate" he said, and pulled Marianne towards him and somehow his lips were on hers and it was so good with her body pressed against him. Her nearness shook him to the core of his being, but the timing was all wrong, he needed to look after his sister! He took a deep breath, and looked into Marianne's bemused eyes, as he heard a sound from Sarah Kate.

"Evan John, what have you to tell me?" Sarah Kate asked, she tried to sit up and her hand went to her chest where it was painful. Evan slowly helped her into a sitting position and piled up the hay behind her, so that she might rest against it.

He didn't know how badly she had been injured, and what that dry cough meant, but he did know that she had to know about Jerome, it might be the catalyst to help make her well! He looked into her disturbed eyes and knew that she had suffered dreadfully before coming to France, and wondered what further traumas he and Jerome would eventually find out about her stay here! He took her hand, and sat back on his heels, already she seemed much better than when they had arrived and had scared her so much.

"Sarah Kate, do you remember when I went missing, and I'd ditched my Spitfire in the sea, and a fishing boat picked me up, it was like a miracle." Evan said watching his sister closely. She had gone very still, and was hardly breathing. "Well, when they told you Jerome was dead, he had been thrown out of the Spitfire when it hit a tree, and it did explode, but Jerome was only slightly burned and concussed." The grip she had on his hand was becoming painful as Sarah listened to his words, almost unable to breath. "When it exploded, Jerome was nowhere near. It took

Jerome a couple of days when he came around to get help, and he was taken to hospital. He was very ill, but as soon as he regained consciousness for the second time he told them who he was. It was too late to contact you, as you had already been sent to France." This wasn't strictly true, but he watched as Sarah Kate tried to assimilate all that he had said. Evan and Marianne watched her carefully and she didn't move for a couple of minutes and Evan wondered if he should have waited until she was well to receive this news! She sat up and stared at Evan John. "Where is my husband, where is Jerome?"

"He has gone to fetch a doctor with Jacques, but he didn't want to go. We didn't want to shock you, you were delirious when we found you, and perhaps we should have waited to tell you when the doctor was here." Evan watched his twin, and saw the news she had received slowly dawn on her, as she started to believe his shocking words, then she slowly smiled and gripped Evan's hand hard, and then turned to Marianne in wonder.

"Marianne can you help me to get cleaned up please, and could you do my hair? I need to get changed Evan, can you go and fetch some water from the river. Evan, I won't see the doctor until I've seen and touched Jerome, I have to know that he is real and not a dream, and I would like to look better than this." She spread out her grubby hands to show them, and then having set things in motion, she reclined in the hay, put her head on her hand, and moved her chest into a more comfortable position. Marianne looked worried, but Evan shook his head slowly. Sarah Kate sighed, maybe she should take one of her Benzedrine pills to keep her awake as she had to see Jerome, and then she closed her eyes.

"Don't worry Marianne, she has fallen asleep, she must need it. I will go and fetch some water, and perhaps you can find Sarah Kate something clean to wear?" Evan said looking proudly at his twin, then towards the few pieces of clothing spread out on the hay.

Later Sarah Kate was listening for the car that would bring Jerome to her. Marianne had helped her to wash and change, she still looked very pale and ill, but there was a strange aura of power about her. She was going to see Jerome the husband that she had believed was lost to her forever in this life. He was coming back to her, the War was over, her family were all well according to her brother, and the doctor would have to wait until she had seen and touched Jerome. She was clean, and the clothes Marianne had helped her into were clean also, but very crumpled after being washed in the river and left to dry in the hay.

They heard the car coming along the cart track, and Evan and Marianne went down the ladder from the top of the hay. Evan and Marianne looked at each other just before the three men arrived through the barn door, Evan snatched a kiss as he was feeling so very relieved and happy, and Marianne shyly kissed him back.

Jerome came into the barn looking anxious and yet fraught and charged, and at a nod from Evan he slowly climbed the ladder, and stepped into the unsteady soft hay which mirrored the way he was feeling. There was a long stretched out moment, as their eyes met, and then Sarah Kate was in his arms, and he struggled not to hurt her bruised body and he felt deliriously happy, something he had not expected to feel again! They had both suffered so much over the weeks, months and years since his plane had gone down in a blazing inferno, but now they were together, and they must put that all behind them. Jerome looked into her beautiful but very tired eyes and sighed, he must take things easily and care for his lovely wife, and then at some time in the future she would let him share her memories. When she was well again he would take her to Canada to see his mother, she would be anxiously waiting to hear from him, as he had been keeping her informed of his movements. He didn't want to move away from Sarah Kate but he was being selfish, she must see the doctor.

Sarah Kate could not believe she deserved such happiness. She slowly moved her hands over her husband's face, then his shoulders and arms, and slowly lifted the shirt off his arms to see his scars. Her eyes filled with tears, she should have been there to look after and comfort him! Jerome wiped the tears away from her eyes with his thumbs, and slowly kissed her lips, promising so much when she was well again.

The doctor paced the barn floor, "Who is this woman I have come to see, dragging me all this way, why didn't you bring her to my office?"

Marianne looked at the doctor, he was from Verneuil, and she wondered if he had already had Violette as a patient.

"Violette Marsaud, you might know her." Marianne said brusquely.

"Why didn't you say, I've treated Mademoiselle Marsaud before. She is a very brave young lady." The Doctor was about to continue, but was stopped.

"Patient confidentiality," Marianne reminded him, she didn't want Sarah Kate's husband and her brother to hear all the frightening details all at once. Sarah Kate could tell them in her own time, *if* she wanted to!

"Doctor would you care to examine my wife," Jerome said from the top of the ladder, which he held firmly for the doctor to climb.

The doctor was very kind and careful with Sarah Kate, as he was now allowed to tend her, and he did not comment on anything except how she felt today! The strapping on her chest, he did with new bandages with the help of Marianne, and he gave her some painkillers, together with medicine to

191

clear her chest, and could not resist a little look at the scar on her thigh, it didn't look too bad! He gave her the all clear with regard to travelling in a few days time, as Jerome insisted that they would get a flight home in due course. Having eaten some food, and taken a satisfying drink, Sarah Kate even managed to climb down the ladder herself, with her husband very close of course.

"Oh dear, there are six of us," Sarah Kate said with a smile. "I suggest we leave Evan and Marianne to walk back to Sainte Pierre." When Jacques looked surprised and about to object, Sarah took his weak arm firmly, he obviously needed things explaining to him.

Jerome watched his wife in amazement, as an hour ago she had been barely conscious, now she was looking after Jacques Flamand! He felt a slight pain in his chest which he thought might be jealousy, and then when she settled in the front of the car beside him, he was pleased to drive as she kept contact with him with her hand on his knee.

As she watched the countryside around her, she thought she would like France, in the future when all the scars of War had healed, but for now she would be going home to England, and then home to the valley of her birth. Tonight they would get a room in Verneuil, and wait for their flight home with the RAF. Marianne and Evan would have time together, and they would let Madame Marsaud at the farm, and Gerrard and Aunt Bridgette know that 'Violette' had been found safe, if not well!

"Please stop the car Jerome," they were passing the Cafe Marsaud, and as she didn't quite feel up to getting out of the car, she asked Jacques to fetch Madame Marsaud and Gerrard outside for a moment. Madame was overcome with joy at seeing Violette again, and was pleased when Violette hugged her, and thanked her 'Aunt Bridgette' for looking after her. Gerrard was about to pull her out of the car to kiss her on both cheeks when he saw how ill she looked. Instead he kissed his fingers and placed them on her forehead. Jerome settled back in his seat, that wasn't too bad for a Frenchman, and he would have his wife all to himself for a couple of days and nights, then he might be prepared to share her with her family and his.

Sarah Kate was thinking about Jerome, but she allowed a memory of Marianne at the Chateau Genevieve to slip through her mind, when she had been forced there by Oberleutnant Schiller the first time. No, she was certain that Marianne was there under the care of Oberst Werner Muller and the Mayor of Verneuil.

Madame Marsaud watched with a deep melancholy as the car was driven away, in her weak state there was absolutely no reason to inform Violette that the body of Jean Distelle had been found, and if her husband and brother had not come looking for her, *she* might *never* have been found.

CHAPTER TWENTY ONE

Sarah Kate was lying on the bed next to her husband who had fallen asleep.

She put out her hand to touch him, just to make sure that he was there and he was real. Even in his sleep his hand closed over hers comfortingly, and she wondered how long it would be before they were able to lead a normal life, instead of always having to know where the other was, and preferably within touching distance!

She stared out of the window of Rowan Trees at the familiar hills in the distance. She felt sublimely happy to be home and yes, safe. It was the middle of the afternoon and she could hear voices downstairs. The house seemed to be forever full, and just now everyone was happy. Particularly her young sister Megs, who had just promised to marry Zeke Williams, and she was looking forward to taking on his two children too.

Evan John would be returning to his RAF base down South in a day or so. He would be flying, and yes they would still worry about his safety, but at least the War was over.

The family had been really wonderful, as they had not badgered her for information about where she had been and what she had been doing. She knew that over the years, at least Evan John and Jerome would learn most of it, but the others including her parents were just pleased to have her home and safe. She wasn't ready yet to impart such knowledge, it was too new and too personal, and yet that time would come eventually she was sure.

She no longer needed the tight bandages around her chest, and soon she hoped that Jerome would stop treating her like an invalid. When she last looked in the mirror she had started to look more like her old self, at least her husband thought so, and he was very supportive. He was arranging for them to visit his home in Canada, and Sarah Kate was looking forward to meeting his mother, but she regretted that his father had died months earlier, and it was too late for her to meet him. Meeting his mother couldn't possibly be as frightening as the last few years could it?

She blushed slightly with pleasure, as she remembered the two nights they had spent in Verneuil, France, after they had found her in the barn. She and Jerome had been sublimely happy and fulfilled to be together again, and had found ways to be as close as they needed even with her injuries, and they had almost resented the news that the plane had arrived to take them home to England.

Sarah had watched with much interest, the effect that Evan John and Marianne had on each other, and she believed that soon Evan John would return to spend some time in Sainte Pierre with that lovely girl, who would always be prized as a close friend by Sarah Kate. It seemed also that Jacques was receiving treatment for his beaten body, and was doing very well, and the Marsaud Bakery was going from strength to strength, and Gerrard often made a point of visiting the Mesdames Marsaud and Distelle at the farm. All

195

this she knew because, as promised, Marianne had written a long informative letter. This she had enclosed in a letter to Evan John, and with that letter to Sarah Kate was another, for Mademoiselle Violette Marsaud. This letter for Violette had been sent care of the Bakery Marsaud.

Sarah fingered the letter, and smiled happily. She had been very pleased and relieved to learn that Herr Werner Muller, had returned to his wife and daughters, and they were all well. Just as he hoped was Mademoiselle Marsaud. He wished her happiness in her future life, and she wished him the same, although she did not have an address to write to. Thinking back over that terrible night in the Chateau, Sarah Kate now believed that Werner must have realised there was more to her than Violette Marsaud, particularly as she had dispatched Schiller with a rather specific type of knife. She sighed remembering him as a real gentleman. If it had not been for each other, there would have been *no life* for either one, or even both, of them to enjoy!

One day soon, she would have much to share with her loving husband, but for now they must enjoy this wonderful time of peace and tranquillity in the wonderful Langdale valley, in the English Lake District in which she had been born, the place she would always call home.

Once again she could lift up her eyes to the familiar hills, and yes, she thought she *had* received help!